Montreal
From
Bread to
Wine

by Phil, Carola
&David Price

Library and Archives Canada Cataloguing in Publication

Price, Phil, 1974-
        Montreal, from bread to wine / Phil Price, Carola Price,
David Price.

"A vivva city guide".
Includes index.
ISBN 1-896881-54-8

        1. Restaurants—Québec (Province)—Montréal—Guidebooks.
I. Price, Carola, 1970- II. Price, David, 1973- III. Title.

TX907.5.C22M6 2005a   647.95714'28   C2005-902076-8

Cover design: I Love Neon/John Hatz
Inside design: Studio Melrose/Ted Sancton

Printed and bound in Canada

Copyright © 2005 Vivva City Guides
Vivva City is a division of:
Price-Patterson Ltd. - Canadian Publishers
Montreal, Canada - www.pricepatterson.com

The Montreal restaurant world is fast-moving and quick to change. This is a good thing for Montrealers and visitors. We have made every effort to verify the information in this guide, but names, locations, owners and menus may change. If it matters, call ahead. If it doesn't and upon in-person inspection a given restaurant, for whatever reason, is no longer suitable for you, you will likely find yourself in a great dining neighbourhood - and Montreal is a great place to discover the unexpected.

Ch. 4 – Nightclubs and Bars

*Contains off-Island of Montreal Listings

Introduction

Montreal is a food town. Our island is brimming with restaurants, representing every culinary corner of the globe. We are
proud eaters, with abundant appetites and discriminating
palates. However, unlike other cities renowned for their food
culture, Montrealers aren't snobs when it comes to their eating.
Food is to be enjoyed, but is taken only as seriously as it needs
to be. In Montreal, a meal isn't a time to fill ourselves with the
requisite energy needed to last the day. We eat with a healthy
balance of necessity, humour and love. It's our idea of what
makes a meal important that allows us to be recognized as a
gourmet town. Montrealers expect a level of excellence in their
dining that fits the meal laid in front of them, be it a perfectly
executed *foie de veau* at a top French outfit, or two eggs over
easy at the local greasy spoon.

At the heart of our food identity is a love of eating, drinking
and the experience that a good meal provides. Montrealers wear
their food experiences like culinary medals. We are maniacally
proud of our secret spots, knowing where to get the best *café
au lait*, burger, baguettes or *steak frites*. Montrealers seek out
these culinary experiences, squirreling them away in the hopes
of proudly showing them off to visiting friends or of trading the
inside dope on where to get the best-of-the-best in exchange for
a culinary epiphany yet to be had. We know what to look for in
a restaurant, in a meal and in our daily routine to keep our bel-
lies filled and our souls happy.

Montrealers even have their own peculiarities when talking
about food. For instance, in Montreal, an 'entrée' usually means
an appetizer – whereas in the rest of the English-speaking world,
the same word means main course. Like 'Quebec English' words
such as autoroute, this usage is probably a loan from the French.
We take pride in our linguistic peculiarities, but we are especial-

ly proud of this one. It does, after all, concern food.

Montreal is rife with good eating. As you walk around our city you can see it on the *terrasses* of Prince Arthur, the bring-your-own-wine spots on Duluth, the *pho* joints in Chinatown, the aisles of the Jean Talon Market or the endless cafés that pepper our city. Our citizens take their food seriously enough to know it has to be easy, enjoyable, good value, of a high standard and fun. This book will serve you as a culinary *Sherpa* helping you to navigate our wonderfully varied gastronomic landscape. Eat well, laugh often and savour every meal.

Rules to eat by

There are rules that can be followed to help ensure pleasurable experiences are had when you go out to grab a bite. Here are a few:

◎ **Never order what you can make at home.** The point of eating out is to *eat out*. Never order anything you often make at home, or – even worse – make at home well. The bulk of the time, this kind of meal will be better coming from your kitchen than from someone else's. In the same vein, if you have ever had a great meal at a specific restaurant after a life-changing experience – meeting the love of your life, your first date with them, your first night with them – don't go looking for that meal at some other restaurant. The new place will never fail to disappoint.

◎ **Always ask.** Waiters are there to guide you through the menu. Ask them what the specialties are, what dish is most ordered, what they like to eat. The waiters will generally tell you the truth. The most ordered dish is generally the best.

◎ **Look around.** Use the time between sitting down and ordering to take a look around at what the other diners are having. Some simple 'recon' work can give you an idea of what to order.

If you are in a Mexican restaurant and the bulk of the patrons are speaking Spanish, it is safe to say that you are in good hands.

◎ **Order wisely.** If you are at an Indian restaurant, don't order the burger. Many diners end up ordering poorly because they want something that's not on the menu or that doesn't belong in the type of restaurant they're in. If you feel like a burger, go to a burger joint. Ethnic restaurants sometimes put mainstream items on their menus to placate less adventurous customers. Don't be this person! There is nothing worse than a dish poorly interpreted by a chef who has no experience making it or no joy in doing so.

◎ **Have fun.** Be adventurous, try everything and enjoy the experience.

Quality indicator

We have all had some horrible experiences in restaurants: they never leave our culinary memory. These stories can be traded (between laughs) with others for years to come, but that doesn't mean we seek them out. There are some key tell-tale signs that differentiate an okay restaurant from a great one. These indicators will allow you to judge almost immediately if a restaurant is up to snuff. As a paying customer, there is an expectation of value that you should impose on any establishment you visit. And restaurants are not only about food. Every facet of a restaurant is dictated by the owner and the chef – and the experience they yearn to give, the food they set out to serve and the world they create define what their place is all about. The signs that they have succeeded are easy to spot.

◎ **Arriving.** Your arrival is the first impression you get of the experience ahead. Once you cross the threshold from the street to the restaurant's universe, you are a guest and should be treated as such. A hostess, waiter, manager, owner or some form of staff should greet you and dote on your arrival. It is, of course, excusable if things are a little slower when the place is packed, however, a simple "I'll be right with you" from any of the staff should be standard. A restaurant that doesn't greet, or – worse – ignores its diners, displays a general attitude about the treatment of its clientele. A great restaurant recognizes your arrival, promptly seats you and makes you feel immediately comfortable and welcome.

◎ **The table.** Whether sitting at the counter of a diner or at the beautifully appointed table of an expensive French restaurant, the place at which you sit is full of clues which will tell whether you're in for delight or disappointment. First and foremost, the table has to be clean. Is there a smudge of old ketchup? Dirty water glasses? Leftover food from the last diners? Is the cutlery clean? The table allows diners to evaluate the experience ahead. Cleanliness is of paramount importance in a restaurant. If they can't keep the tables clean, how well do they treat the food they are about to serve you? Cleanliness has nothing to do with price. Some of the cleanest establishments are the cheapest. Due to high turnover, they have to maintain a maniacal eye on sanitation. Once seated, check out the space you are eating in. If the cutlery is clean, the table is well set and the glasses are free of marks, then it's safe to assume you are in good hands.

◎ **Music.** The atmosphere of the restaurant affects the experience. If the music booming through the speakers is too loud, obnoxious or unsuitable for the setting, it indicates that the management has not given sufficient thought to the restaurant's mood. Not a good sign for the hours (or minutes) ahead.

◎ **Service.** The service you receive through the course of your meal is another pointer that allows you to gauge the overall quality of the place. Everyone has suffered at the hands of a nasty waiter. The waiter is a representative of the establishment and reflects the attitude of the owner. If the waiter doesn't care about you, the owner feels the same way or has failed to execute on his vision. Service does, and should, vary. If you are at a pub eating a burger, expect pub service. If you are paying for a very expensive meal, expect commensurate service. Nevertheless, *all* waiters should be attentive, courteous, polite and eager to serve you. Bad service, regardless of the establishment, should never be tolerated. If you have a reasonable problem with your waiter, don't leave a tip and explain why to the manager. Bad behaviour should never be rewarded. Restaurant-goers rarely complain about bad service – and this is absolutely wrong. Some people fear reprisals from wait staff through food tampering. The likelihood of food tampering is equal to the chances of getting attacked by a shark while driving your car.

◎ **Bread and water.** Once seated, diners should receive a glass of water. The water should be cold and in a clean glass. Once you've ordered, a basket of complimentary bread should be brought to your table. Generally, restaurants bring bread after you've ordered: bringing it before might affect what your order. The bread is the first taste from the kitchen. If you get stale bread with packets of runny, melted butter, you are in trouble. If you get fresh slices of baguette or good quality bread with fresh butter, it demonstrates that the right amount of thought has been put into that first bite. Bread is cheap and easy to serve fresh. Any place that misses this small detail might also be missing the bigger picture.

◎ **Bathrooms.** The bathroom of a restaurant is indicative of the establishment's attitude towards cleanliness. If the bathrooms are clean, every facet of the restaurant will likely adhere to that standard. If they are filthy, the entire place may suffer under the same, wrong approach. This is a golden rule that is rarely wrong.

◎ **Timing.** Once you have ordered your food, the wait should be roughly 15 to 20 minutes for your entrées. This will allow you and your fellow diners to settle in, enjoy your wine and build up a slight appetite for your order. Waiting any longer than half an hour for your entrée is ridiculous. Your main course should also arrive within a 10- to 20-minute window after your entrée. Desserts should take a little longer to allow for digestion and build up a sense of excitement for the final bow from the kitchen.

◎ **Food temperature.** Apart from quality, which always varies between establishments, temperature is important. Hot food should be just that, hot. If hot food is served tepid, it means that it has been waiting at the pass in the kitchen for the server. Tepid, lukewarm food is evidence of the establishment's (poor) organization.

◎ **Coffee.** Along with bread and bathrooms, coffee is a good, quick test of a restaurant's quality. Coffee is the curtain call, the final parting taste of the establishment. It's such a small, easily controlled aspect of the dining experience. Terrible, truck stop-style coffee shows the owners didn't think about the final impression. Great coffee demonstrates a sense of forethought and pride.

A word about our categories, areas & indices

The content of the bring-your-own-wine and terrasse chapters is self-explanatory. The $15-30 chapter and the price ranges in the bring-your-own-wine and terrasse chapters indicate what a main dish likely costs at the included establishments. There may be options above and below this range. For a full listing of Montreal restaurants, visit our website www.vivvamontreal.com.

We have tried to create geographical areas that are helpful. No one goes out to dinner and says, "I must eat inside the boundaries of Outremont/Mile End/St. Laurent – come what may," but they do have an idea of where they want to go and what is close to them. Some of our areas (e.g. the Plateau) are walkable and tend to be covered on foot. As a result, they are quite small. Others tend to be covered by car and so are quite large. Here is the key to our areas (see also map, inside front cover):

Mount Royal – Snowdon, Côte des Neiges, Town of Mount Royal, Outremont, Little Italy

Downtown: Downtown, Chinatown

Old Montreal: Old Montreal, Park Jean Drapeau

Plateau: Plateau Mont Royal, Mile End

North End: (former town of) St. Laurent, Ahuntsic, Villeray, Park Extension, Montreal North

South End: Lasalle, Verdun, Ville Emard, St. Henri, Point St. Charles

East End: St. Leonard, Anjou, Montreal East, Rosemont, Petit Patrie, Hochelaga-Maisonneuve

West End: Côte St. Luc, NDG, Westmount

Laval & North Shore: Laval, Rosemere, St. Thérèse, Candiac, Hudson

South Shore: Chateauguay, La Prairie, Brossard, Greenfield Park, Longueuil, St. Lambert, St. Hubert, Chambly, Boucher-ville, St. Jean sur Richelieu

West Island: St. Anne de Bellevue, Baie d'Urfé, Kirkland, Pierre-fonds, Beaconsfield, Dollard des Ormeaux, Pointe Claire, Dorval, Lachine

Nun's Island.

When there are 'off-Island of Montreal' restaurants in a given section (e.g. 'Chinese' or 'Italian'), we have split the section into two or three, as needed: Island of Montreal; Laval & North Shore; and South Shore.

To make restaurants that you know (or that you want to find out about) easy to locate in the book, we have three indices:

1.   Restaurants alphabetically (p. 168)
2.   Restaurants organized by area (p. 176)

Chapter 1.
Bring-Your-Own-Wine Restaurants

In the early 70's, restaurants in Montreal were opening at a furious pace all over the island. The liquor commission had a hard time keeping up with permit demand and a moratorium on issuing new licenses to eating establishments was instituted to curb the growth. The Greeks, in their infinite wisdom, introduced a radical idea: a restaurant where the customer brings his own wine. It was an instant success. Montreal has over 100 bring-your-own-wine spots, covering a broad spectrum of culinary styles and ranging in price from affordable BYOWs (bring-your-own-wines) to *haute gamme cuisine* which could easily (and do) compete with Montreal's best, fully licensed restaurants.

Montrealers love a good deal and budget-minded foodies who yearned for great dining experiences, but couldn't stand the mark-up on wine, were blessed with this innovation. Normally, restaurants mark-up their liquor prices, especially bottles of wine, anywhere from 50 to 300 percent of the wholesale cost. It is always frustrating to pay $40 for a wine you know you can pick up from the liquor store for $15 a bottle. A nice dinner for two can quickly become expensive with wine at these price levels. At a BYOW, great food can still be had for a reasonable price and you can bring that old bottle of wine gathering dust on your kitchen counter, a relic from some long past dinner party.

As an added bonus, BYOW places provide a casual and fun atmosphere. A large group of friends can gather for a nice long meal and each bring a bottle of wine. Everyone almost always brings a different bottle, whether purchased at a *dépanneur* or brought from home. This wide variety of different wines allows all at the table to try something new, discover new wines and broaden their palates. The BYOW restaurant makes a night out cheaper, more communal and informal.

The BYOW arrangement works well for restaurants, too. A restaurant is a difficult, expensive and time-consuming endeavour, and permits, bar costs and added expenses of every imaginable kind present themselves the moment liquor is implicated in the day-to-day operation. For owners, the BYOW revolution has been great. It reduced these operating costs tremendously and allowed them to concentrate on their food and the experience they try to offer to their patrons.

Neighbourhoods

PRINCE ARTHUR

The heart of the bring-your-own-wine culture is Prince Arthur (between St. Laurent/St. Lawrence Boulevard and Laval). The bulk of BYOW restaurants on Prince Arthur are Greek: **Casa Grecque** (p. 29), **Caverne Grecque** (p. 29), **Gourmet Grecque** (p. 29), **Cabane Grecque** (p. 29) and **Le Prince Arthur** (p. 30). If you are meeting people at any Greek joint on Prince Arthur make sure you get the name and address right!

There is a *dépanneur* (or dep) on Prince Arthur (just east of St. Laurent, north side of the street). You can buy domestic beer; some imported beers and a variety of lower-end wine at deps, although for better wine it is best to go to a Société des Alcools du Québec. Bring-your-own-wines used to be just that, but many now permit beer. You'd definitely be pushing your luck if you cracked open a bottle of tequila and started doing shots.

Prince Arthur is an amazing street and has a lot more to offer than just food – even though that's enough for most people. On summer nights, the street is closed to traffic and a number of street performers entertain the public. They range from the good to the breathtakingly talented. You'll soon find an act for you. The restaurants are generally completely packed and getting a table outside can be a medium to long wait on Thursday, Friday and Saturday nights. But in the heavy air of a lazy summer night, the murmur of good times swirling around you and a lilting jazz riff banged out on the guitar of a talented busker, waiting doesn't feel all that bad.

The establishments on Prince Arthur range from fair to exceptional. The quality of ingredients and freshness is excellent due to the sheer amount of volume BYOW places manage to do. The kitchens are in excellent condition and are used to high turnover. After your meal, take a walk through Square St. Louis, a picturesque park at the eastern end of Prince Arthur Street.

DULUTH

Duluth is another hot spot for bring-your-own-wine. Firstly, there is the eponymous **Au Vieux Duluth** (p. 32). This restaurant began on Duluth, but has since opened branches throughout Montreal. Duluth, like Prince Arthur, is a BYOW destination with several restaurants covering a variety of cooking styles. Duluth has a greater number of Italian BYOWs and also has fewer line-ups than Prince Arthur. There are several dep's on Duluth, as well as a SAQ Express (see below for a description) on the northeastern corner of St. Denis Street.

Bring-your-Own-Wine Fare

The food served at bring-your-own-wine establishments ranges from fair to exquisite. Bring-your-own-wine dining is generally more about the overall experience than the cuisine. The culinary styles in the BYOW universe heavily favour continental Italian and Greek fare.

A WORD ABOUT CHOOSING AND FINDING YOUR WINE

The *Société des Alcools du Québec* (or 'SAQs'/'Sacks', as its branches are affectionately called) carries an assortment of wine. This chain is the provincial liquor monopoly. It is the only place to buy many imported beers, all hard alcohol and better wines. In recent years, it has transformed itself from a sleepy government department to an aggressive modern retailer. The majority of its wine selection is French, ranging in price from $10 to $50. Legally, you are able to buy liquor in Quebec from 9:30 am in the morning until 10 pm at night (11 pm at a dep), but you must a find a store that is open and caters to your taste and needs. There are three varieties of SAQ to choose from. The **Express** is open early and closes late. It offers a regular selection of wine, beer and spirits. There are not many new or exciting wines offered here, but the old standby is often just what is needed. The next is the **Classique**. This store has more regular hours, but often stays open late Thursday and Friday. The premium selections and a variety of wines from around the world are found here. The price range can be staggering, depending on the neighbourhood in which the store is located. It is at a Classique where the SAQ becomes a business entity, catering to all of its clients' needs and wishes. The last is the **Selection** at which there are regular products, wine show selections and higher-priced, hard-to-stock items, such as a vintage port from the early 80's and a bottle of champagne from the 2000 vintage.

Whatever help you need, the staff at the SAQ is always there to help. There are many consultants on staff with extensive wine training. Bring your menu or budget to them and they will help you in a friendly and efficient manner. They taste almost every product that comes into their store and, as such, are always on the lookout for great bargains and new and exciting finds from all over the world.

Remember that Quebec leans a bit too much towards France, so unless you have a specific need, ask the staff members if there is something they have enjoyed that is local. It will help broaden your horizons – and Canadian selections have recently been winning awards, both here and abroad.

ITALIAN
Food

At the Italian places, look for pastas accompanied with the traditional slate of sauces, pizzas and classic veal dishes (e.g. *marsala, parmiagiano, picatta*). For an appetizer, you will find that standards such as *bruschetta,* Caeser salad and *prosciutto e melone* are generally well executed. Instead of the traditional spaghetti with tomato or meat sauce, try a spicy *puttanesca*, a savoury sauce comprised of olives, garlic, anchovies and capers. It has a nice spicy kick. Avoid heavily creamed sauces, they generally guarantee indigestion and the cream steals from the flavour of the dish. Italians are masters of simple flavours and they do wonders with fresh ingredients. Make sure you are able to enjoy them.

Tiramisu is the dessert of choice. It is interpreted differently on every Italian dessert menu, depending on the chef, which town he is from in Italy and, most importantly, how his mother prepared it. Some are homemade, others store-bought – it all depends on the restaurant. A good *tiramisu* is a toothsome mix of rich espresso, thick mascarpone cream, finished with a dusting of cocoa powder or chocolate shavings. The *tiramisu* should be firm, served cold and savoured. If you are lucky enough to taste a great *tiramisu,* your life will be complete.

Wine for Italian Food

Quebecers have a fondness for Italian wines and there is always a good section at any SAQ. Like Italian food, Italian wines tend to have a lot of bold red fruit and herbaceous overtones. It is typical to find sour cherries, oregano and fennel in the nose of a good medium- to heavy-bodied red wine. The whites tend to be similar, in that there is a lot of herb and grassy character in the nose and mouth. When enjoying an Italian meal, it is best to start with a sparkling wine such as Moscato d'Asti. It has a delicate sweet flavour with enough bubbles to delight the palate.

When the main course comes, move onto Chianti Classico or the heavier *Sangiovese/Cabernet*-based table wines in the $20-40 range. These wines have a sweet and slightly smoky aftertaste that stays in the mouth for a minute or so. They hold up to veal dishes and tomato-based sauces, with alcohol and oak in every sip.

Grilled vegetables and the nutty and peppery flavours of olive oil bring out the cedar and dark cherry notes in a classic Tuscan *IGT (Indicazione Geographica Tipica)*. This is an indication of what the area makes wine taste like. Regardless of the producer, it will always be typical of the area.

GREEK

Food

The Greek bring-your-own-wine restaurants also range in quality from fair to excellent. Brochettes of chicken, meat or seafood can be found on almost every menu. Always accompanied by rice, potatoes/fries and/or vegetables, all are usually well prepared. The seafood is always the best bet and generally the best value for the dollar. Crab legs, lobster tails and grilled shrimp feature heavily on the menu, accompanied with the requisite amount of garlic butter. Avoid menu items such as steaks that aren't indigenous to Greek cuisine. (An even worse offender: pizza.)

Certain restaurants feature an array of specials that go from 2-for-1s to all-inclusive table d'hôtes. Experimentation is the key. Most Montrealers choose their preferred bring-your-own Greek restaurant and remain utterly loyal, even if it may not be the best in the city. We would advise against this habit, but less than stellar food is easily forgivable if you're out on the *terrasse,* sipping good wine with great friends.

Wine for Greek Food

There hasn't been much action on the shelves for Greek

wines, but the SAQ has started to pick up on the quality of the country's wines. It is now offering clients a myriad of red and white wines. When dining at a Greek restaurant, enjoy a light bodied Boutari red. It has a slightly jammy character and will play off the lemon and oregano coating of fish beautifully. If white is more appealing, stay away from the Retsina and move to Kouros Patras. Retsina is a good choice when drinking on a terrasse with traditional mezze, but due to the overwhelming Pine Sol flavour, it may not suit many main dishes. A New Zealand or Australian Sauvignon Blanc works well with fish, but, when ordering the grilled meats, choose a Chardonnay or a red from the Rhone or Pays d'Oc regions of France. Their vegetal and slightly smokey flavours match with the charred taste of the meats.

THE NICHE PLAYERS

Apart from the hot spots mentioned above, there are bring-your-own-wine places all over the island of Montreal, the bulk of which are destination restaurants known for their excellent menus, innovative styles and brilliant chefs. Foodies with an appreciation for cutting-edge cuisine tend to flock to these places. They usually bring very expensive wines from their own collections and eat a fantastic meal paired with a fantastic wine, and they don't have to blow wads of cash.

The small, off-the-beaten-path bring-your-own-wine spots are some of Montreal's best-kept secrets. These adventurous chefs and owners have benefited most from the BYOW phenomenon and use the time freed up by not managing liquor to concentrate on the quality of their service and produce. The cuisine ranges in style, but the majority of these out-of-the-way bring-your-owns are rooted in classic French cuisine. Many take French cuisine to a new level, fusing their own creativity and love of Quebec produce to create new and exciting dishes that amaze and excite the palate. Imaginations run wild and menus can be eclectic, daunting and, almost always, exciting. It takes an adventurous spirit to sift through a handful of these small bring-your-own-wines, but the journey is worthwhile.

Among the noteworthy are **The Flambard** (p. 27), which has become a stand-by for many who enjoy BYOW dining. The trout and the pâté alone are worth the visit. It is an intimate place that is great for group dinners of 20 or less. **Micheal W.** (p. 27) serves a hefty veal chop in a quiet setting. **Beurre Noisette** (p. 26) serves traditional bistro fare and has good meals at reasonable prices. **Le Pégase** (p. 28) is always packed and has amazing coffee. **Lélé de Cuca** (p. 31), a tiny place that is always full, serves great food, including chicken with black beans and rice that makes you feel like you're in Mexico. **Couscous Royal** (p. 32) has wonderful lamb and exceptional couscous. **Poisson Rouge** (p. 32) is great for really fresh fish with standard sides and a great price-to-portion ratio. **Yoyo** (p. 26) is another French BYOW favorite with an amazing cheese plate and great classics like *bavette* and *crème brûlée*. **Après le Jour** (p. 26), another great BYOW, is a little more expensive but very good. The tartares are worth a taste. **Les Délices de l'Île Maurice** (p. 30) is another great spot, cheap and delicious. The chef is a joker who comes out of the kitchen to take your order. Others to visit are: **La Colombe** (north African-influenced, p. 27), **la Raclette** (traditional Swiss, p. 33), **Vents du Sud** (Basque, p. 28) and **P'tit Plateau** (French, p. 28).

At these niche BYOWs, many culinary experiences can be enjoyed and savoured. When in doubt, ask around and those generous enough to share their 'intel' may point you in the right direction. Like the pubs of Ireland, the cafés of Paris and the beer halls of Munich, bring-your-own-wine restaurants are uniquely and singularly Montreal.

Best BYOWs

- Best BYOW for a romantic meal: **Yoyo** (p. 26)
- Best BYOW with terrasse: Any place on Prince Arthur
- Best French: **P'tit Plateau** (p. 28)
- Best Italian: **La Trattoria** (p. 31), not to be confused with the non-BYOW 'Trattoria'
- Best for large groups: **L'Académie** (p. 26)
- Best hidden gem: **Le Flambard** (p. 27)
- Best for birthdays: **Après le Jour** (p. 26)

@ *Afghan*

KHYBER PASS

506 Duluth East, Plateau
(514) 844-7131
Authentic Afghan cuisine. Try
their mantoo, their sambosa as
an entrée, their chopan kebab
(lamb) and the other various
specialities of the house. Typical
decor with several Afghan
photographs and tapestries. Very
friendly owner. Bring your own
wine.

@ *Algerian*

RITES BERBÈRES

4697 de Bullion, Plateau
(514) 844-7863   *$15 to $30*
Specialties include an assortment
of aperitifs, méchoui (Quebec
lamb) and house-made couscous
served with three kinds of meats.
Two rooms. In business for over
18 years. Bring your own wine.

@ *Bistro*

YOYO

4720 Marquette, Plateau
(514) 524-4187   *$15 to $30*
Fine French cuisine. Specialties:
veal and lamb sweetbreads. Bring
your own wine. Capacity of 70.
Cordial ambiance. Sober decor.

@ *French*

ISLAND OF MONTREAL

ACADÉMIE (L')

4051 St. Denis, Plateau
(514) 849-2249   *$15 to $30*
French and Italian cuisine. Cordial
ambiance. Lunch and dinner table
d'hôte that includes soup, salad,
main dish and coffee. Affordable
prices. Bring your own wine.

APRÈS LE JOUR

901 Rachel East, Plateau
(514) 527-4141   *$30 to $45*
French cuisine. Plush ambiance,
bar lounge-style with jazz music.
Try their rice and their veal
kidneys. Homemade desserts.
Reception room. Capacity of 120
clients. Bring your own wine.

BEURRE NOISETTE

4354 Christophe Colomb,
Plateau
(514) 596-2205   *$15 to $30*
Nestled within a quiet residential
neighbourhood, this small, cozy
restaurant is worth discovering.
The menu consists of traditional
French cuisine (cheese plates,
veal, duck, crème brulée, etc.) at
a reasonable price and is served
by a friendly and helpful staff.
Bring your own wine, but if you
happen to forget, there is a
dépanneur right next door.

BISTRO DU ROY (LE)

3784 de Mentana, Plateau
(514) 525-1624   *$15 to $30*
Fine French cuisine specializing in meat offals, game meats, filet mignon and other traditional dishes. Beautiful environment, ideal for outings between friends. Brunches. Bring your own wine.

COLOMBE (LA)

554 Duluth East, Plateau
(514) 849-8844   *$15 to $30*
French cuisine. Entirely nonsmoking. Intimate ambiance. French specialties with a varied menu. Capacity of 36. Closed on Mondays. Bring your own wine.

DALI MATISSE

900 Duluth East, Plateau
(514) 845-6557   *$15 to $30*
French and international cuisine. Try their game meat triad (stag, pheasant, ostrich), the skate and paella of Valencia. Seats 50. Terrasse of 20 places open in the summer. Cordial decor; bistro ambiance.

DÉCOUVERTE (LA)

4350 de La Roche, Plateau
(514) 529-8377   *$15 to $30*
Fine restaurant specializing in filet of lamb, calf brains and duck. Friendly and casual decor. Capacity of 50. Table d'hôte is served only at night. Bring your own wine.

FLAMBARD (LE)

851 Rachel East, Plateau
(514) 596-1280   *$15 to $30*
Small local French restaurant specializing in cassoulet, confit of duck and rack of lamb. Capacity of 40 clients. Friendly ambiance. Open every day. Bring your own wine.

FLOCON (LE)

540 Duluth East, Plateau
(514) 844-0713   *$15 to $30*
Restaurant of 75 places. Sophisticated decor but cordial ambiance. Table d'hôte in the evenings. Different menu each month. Open for over 20 years. Bring your own wine.

HÉRITIERS (LES)

5091 de Lanaudière, Plateau
(514) 528-4953   *$15 to $30*
Restaurant specializing in meat offals. Menu à la carte only and menus for small groups are available. Casual ambiance. Bring your own wine.

MICHAEL W.

2601 Centre, South End
(514) 931-0821   *$15 to $30*
Franco-Italian restaurant specializing in game meats. Try their pears, the ceviche and their crème brûlée. Beautiful terrasse. Four dining rooms with a total capacity of 75 clients. Pleasant and intimate ambiance. Bring your own wine.

P'TIT PLATEAU (LE)

330 Marie Anne East, Plateau
(514) 282-6342
Specialty: dishes from the south-western part of France.
Traditional ambiance. Closed in July.

PETIT RESTO (AU)

4650 de Mentana, Plateau
(514) 598-7963   *$15 to $30*
Specialties: duck liver pâté, confit of duck, hazelnut lamb and filet mignon with blue Ermite sauce. Capacity of 45 clients. Reservations are preferable. Table d'hôte changes each week. Open for over 17 years. Bring your own wine.

PITON DE LA FOURNAISE (LE)

835 Duluth East, Plateau
(514) 526-3936   *$15 to $30*
Exotic cuisine. Restaurant specializes in gastronomy from Reunion Island. Menu has an Indian and African influence. Picturesque and cordial. Open only in the evenings. Bring your own wine.

PRUNELLE (LA)

327 Duluth East, Plateau
(514) 849-8403   *$15 to $30*
Fine French cuisine. Warm and distinguished environment. Large sliding doors that open on Duluth Street in the summer. Bring your own wine.

PÉGASE (LE)

1831 Gilford, Plateau
(514) 522-0487   *$15 to $30*
Small restaurant of 34 places. Gourmet menu includes a soup, a salad, an entrée, the main dish, the dessert and a coffee. Calm ambiance during the week and animated on weekends. Bring your own wine.

LAVAL & NORTH SHORE

ACADÉMIE (L')

1730 Pierre Péladeau, Laval
(450) 988-1015   *$15 to $30*
French and Italian cuisine. Bring your own wine. Welcoming ambiance. Table d'hôte during lunch and dinner that includes soup, salad, main dish and coffee. Affordable prices. Bring your own wine.

ESCARGOT FOU (L')

5303 Blvd. Lévesque, Laval
(450) 664-3105   *$15 to $30*
Restaurant specializing in mussels. Cordial ambiance spread out on two floors. Includes a reception room of 50 places. Bring your own wine.

VENTS DU SUD

323 Roy East, Plateau
(514) 281-9913
Market-style cuisine offering a traditional French menu. Generous portions. Ideal for customers who like homemade cooking. Divided into two rooms.

VIEILLE HISTOIRE (LA)

284 Blvd. St. Rose, Laval
(450) 625-0379   *$15 to $30*
French cuisine with a menu which
changes each season. Bring your
own wine. Good selection of
game meats and meat offals.
Serene atmosphere. Two rooms:
one with 20 seats and another of
40 seats. Interior court yard.
Open every day starting at 6 pm.

© *Greek*

ISLAND OF MONTREAL

CABANE GRECQUE

102 Prince Arthur East,
Plateau
(514) 849-0122   *$15 to $30*
Large, two-floor Greek
restaurant. Higher quality but at
a reasonable price. Excellent
seafood. Bring your own wine.

CASA GRECQUE

200 Prince Arthur East,
Plateau
(514) 842-6098   *$15 to $30*
Excellent place for eating well at
a moderate price. Table d'hôte
starting at $15. Lunch menu for
as little as $5. Children eat for
free from Sunday to Thursday.
Mediterranean dishes that will
keep you coming back for more!
Bring your own wine.

CASA GRECQUE

3855A, St. John's Blvd., West
Island
(514) 626-6626

CASA GRECQUE

5787 Sherbrooke St. East,
East End
(514) 899-5373

CASA GRECQUE

7218 Blvd. Newman, South
End
(514) 364-0494

*See also Laval & North Shore
and South Shore, below.*

CAVERNE GRECQUE

105 Prince Arthur East,
Plateau
(514) 844-5114   *$15 to $30*
Great establishment on two
floors. Up-to-date Greek cuisine
of higher quality. Specialties:
brochettes, steaks and seafood.
Bring your own wine.

GOURMET GREC

180 Prince Arthur East,
Plateau
(514) 849-1335   *$15 to $30*
Specializing in authentic Greek
cuisine and seafood. Dishes start
for as little as $7 and go up to
$25. Bring your own wine.

JARDIN DE PANOS
521 Duluth East, Plateau
(514) 521-4206   *$15 to $30*
Charming restaurant specializing
in brochettes and moderately
priced seafood. Typical Greek
decor. Bring your own wine.

PRINCE ARTHUR (LE)
54 Prince Arthur East, Plateau
(514) 849-2454
Greek cuisine specializing in
brochettes and seafood. Dishes
are between $8 and $30. Try
their prawns, an out of the
ordinary delight.

LAVAL & NORTH SHORE

CASA GRECQUE
1565 Daniel Johnson, Laval
(450) 663-1031
Excellent place for eating well at
a moderate price. Table d'hôte
starting at $15. Lunch menu for
as little as $5. Children eat for
free from Sunday to Thursday.
Mediterranean dishes that will
keep you coming back for more!
Bring your own wine.

CASA GRECQUE
259 Blvd. Labelle, St. Thérèse
(450) 979-4619

CASA GRECQUE
852 Blvd. des Seigneurs,
Laval
(450) 492-2888

CASA GRECQUE
574 Blvd. Arthur Sauvé, Laval
(450) 974-2929

SOUTH SHORE

CASA GRECQUE
8245-A, Taschereau Blvd.,
Brossard
(450) 443-0323
Excellent place for eating well at
a moderate price. Table d'hôte
starting at $15. Lunch menu for
as little as $5. Children eat for
free from Sunday to Thursday.
Mediterranean dishes that will
keep you coming back for more!
Bring your own wine.

CASA GRECQUE
690 de Montbrun,
Boucherville
(450) 449-2249

CASA GRECQUE
3094 ch. de Chambly,
Longueuil
(450) 646-2228

© International

TERRASSE LAFAYETTE
250 Villeneuve West, Plateau
(514) 288-3915   *$15 to $30*
Cordial ambiance with a summer
terrasse. Large variety: French,
Canadian, Italian and Greek
cuisine. Buy three small pizzas
and the fourth one is free.
Bring your own wine.

DÉLICES DE L'ÎLE MAURICE
272 Hickson, South End
(514) 768-6023 *Under $15*
Small restaurant specialized in
Hindu, Chinese and Creole

cuisine. Intimate ambiance, home style decor. Bring your own wine.

◉ *Italian*

ISLAND OF MONTREAL

FORNARINA (LA)
6825 St. Laurent Blvd.
(St. Lawrence), Mount Royal
(514) 271-1741   *$15 to $30*
Family atmosphere with a reception room of 30 to 70 people. Specialized in pizzas cooked in a wood oven. Table d'hôte offered only during lunch. Bring your own wine.

LA TRATTORIA
5563 Upper Lachine Road
(514) 484-5303   *$15 to $30*
Far from Little Italy but a wonderful Italian restaurant. Fine selection of pasta in a wine cellar atmosphere.

LA TRATTORIA
1551 Notre Dame West
(514) 935-5050   *$15 to $30*

LOMBARDI
411 Duluth East, Plateau
(514) 844-9419   *$15 to $30*
Fine cuisine. Restaurant specializes in homemade pasta, seafood and meats. Table d'hôte offered during lunch and dinner. Caring staff. Bring your own wine.

TONY DU SUD
25 Fairmount West, Plateau
(514) 274-7339   *$15 to $30*
Small family restaurant, excellent for family outings and for special occasions. Excellent value. Home-style cuisine. Menu changes often. Bring your own wine.

SOUTH SHORE

ROMA ANTIQUA (LA)
4900 Taschereau Blvd.,
Greenfield Park
(450) 672-2211   *$15 to $30*
Good value. Family ambiance. Good selection of dishes. Bring your own wine. Excellent entrées, like the fried calamari. Try the pasta trio.

◉ *Latin American*

LAS PALMAS PUPUSERIA
632 Jarry East, North End
(514) 270-7334   *$15 to $30*
Salvadorian restaurant. Bring your own wine. Specialties: pupusas, tacos, burritos and grilled meats. Simple selection offering generous portions.

LÉLÉ DE CUCA
70 Marie Anne East, Plateau
(514) 849-6649   *$15 to $30*
Small intimate restaurant that serves generous portions of chicken and seafood. Bring your own wine. Capacity of 40. Nonsmoking establishment. Open for over 22 years.

◎ *Mediterranean*

TOUCHEH
351 Prince Albert, West End
(514) 369-6868   *$15 to $30*
Specialties: Mediterranean and
Iranian cuisine. Exotic ambiance
and decor. Varied menu, several
Mediterranean, Iranian and
European dishes. Always fresh
ingredients. Bring your own wine.

◎ *Morrocan*

COUSCOUS ROYAL
919 Duluth East, Plateau
(514) 528-1307   *$15 to $30*
Traditional Moroccan cuisine.
Specialties: couscous and
barbecue lamb. Table d'hôte
includes an entrée, main dish and
mint tea. Bring your own wine.

◎ *Seafood*

POISSON ROUGE (LE)
1201 Rachel East, Plateau
(514) 522-4876   *$15 to $30*
Large restaurant located opposite
Lafontaine Park. Ideal for all
special occasions. Table d'hôte at
$32. Excellent quality/price ratio.
Bring your own wine.

◎ *Steak House*

ISLAND OF MONTREAL

VIEUX DULUTH (AU)
12856 Sherbrooke St. East,
East End
(514) 498-4886   *$15 to $30*
Renowned for their generous
portions, excellent value and
impeccable service. The largest
restaurant chain that serves
grilled meats and seafood in
Quebec. Ideal for family outings,
or for outings of friends or
groups. Children's menu is
available. Bring your own wine.

VIEUX DULUTH (AU)
1997 Blvd. Marcel Laurin,
North End
(514) 745-4525   *$15 to $30*

VIEUX DULUTH (AU)
351 Duluth East, Plateau
(514) 842-5390   *$15 to $30*

VIEUX DULUTH (AU)
3610 St. John's Blvd., West
Island
(514) 624-0350   *$15 to $30*

VIEUX DULUTH (AU)
5100 Sherbrooke St. East,
East End
(514) 254-1347   *$15 to $30*

VIEUX DULUTH (AU)
5600 Blvd. Henri Bourassa
East, North End
(514) 326-7381   *$15 to $30*

*See also Laval & North Shore
and South Shore, below.*

LAVAL & NORTH SHORE

VIEUX DULUTH (AU)
999 Blvd. St. Martin West,
Laval
(450) 629-1611   *$15 to $30*
Renowned for their generous
portions, excellent quality/price

value and impeccable service. The largest restaurant chain that serves grilled meats and seafood in Quebec. Ideal for family outings, or for outings of friends or groups. Children's menu is available. Bring your own wine.

SOUTH SHORE

VIEUX DULUTH (AU)
3902 Taschereau Blvd., Greenfield Park
(450) 672-9921   *$15 to $30*
Renowned for their generous portions, excellent quality/price value and impeccable service. The largest restaurant chain that serves grilled meats and seafood in Quebec. Ideal for family outings, or for outings of friends or groups. Children's menu is available. Bring your own wine.

Swiss

RACLETTE (LA)
1059 Gilford, Plateau
(514) 524-8118   *$15 to $30*
Swiss and European style cuisine. Specialties: Fondue and raclette. Large variety of European dishes: duck, scallops, filet mignon, etc. Small and large table d'hôte, private room and a summer terrasse.

Thai

THAI-VIET
3610 St. Dominique, Plateau
(514) 288-5577   *$15 to $30*
Fine Vietnamese and Thai cuisine. A diverse menu includes soups, grilled meats, noodles and other dishes. Terrasse with a capacity of 80 people open during the summer. Typical Asian decor. Bring your own wine.

Vietnamese

HARMONIE D'ASIE (L')
65 Duluth East, Plateau
(514) 289-9972   *$15 to $30*
Open for over 15 years. Menu includes imperial rolls and spring rolls, vegetarian dishes and several soups. Open from 5 pm to 10 pm. Bring your own wine.

Chapter 2. Terrasses

In Montreal, a 'terrasse' (never a 'terrace') is anywhere a restaurant owner can find 2 feet of usable sidewalk. (To verify this theory, check out the very small, but serviceable terrasse at **Upstairs** (p. 49) on Mackay below St. Catherine.) The aggressive use of sidewalk space is not the only way that Montrealers push the limits of the possible. Montrealers are notoriously outdoorsy come summertime. After a winter of cabin fever who can blame us? This manifests itself in the terrasse phenomenon. With great enthusiasm, we bound into spring, generally prematurely, and spend the next five months almost exclusively outdoors. The minute an ounce of snow melts, someone, somewhere will be out on a terrasse – even if it's only for a minute and a half at high noon, basking in that little whisper of sun that begins to melt away the memory of winter. Later in the year, Montrealers will spend hours on terrasses, storing up sunrays for the coming winter. Terrasses can be found in every corner of the city. Tables are haphazardly set up at the end of March outside cafés and restaurants of all kinds (until a horrid blizzard unloads in mid-April). Some terrasses are small configurations of bistro tables on a sidewalk; others are little undiscovered oases at the back of restaurants. Some are delightfully hidden courtyards glowing by candlelight, others are huge mega-terrasses packed with tourists. Whatever the state of a terrasse, food always seems to taste a little better outside.

Terrasses are generally the hottest real estate for restaurant-goers. When making reservations, make sure to specify your preference (in or outdoors). During the warm summer months, terrasses are always full. Terrasses are all over town and are not specific to a particular neighborhood. However, there are terrasse-heavy areas throughout Montreal. In terms of season, terrasses can start as early as March and some establishments push the season until the end of October. Again, Canadian optimism tends to win out regardless of environmental realities.

Neighbourhoods

McGill College

McGill College is the central street of downtown Montreal. On one end are McGill University and Mount Royal; on the other, Place Ville Marie – still the premiere office tower 43 years after its was finished in 1962. From a pedestrian and restaurant-goer's point of view, the street has improved greatly over the last 20 years. Trees have been planted in the median. In summer, they add some green to the street's ambiance and offer the prospect (if not the fulfillment) of coolness. In winter, they are decorated with Christmas lights and help to chase away the winter blues. Obviously, for the terrasse section of a restaurant guide, it is *summer* that will concern people most. McGill College does not disappoint in this regard. At noon (and after), the sun is in the west, on the right-hand side looking down from McGill University. As a result, the best sites for catching some sunshine are on the east (left hand) side. There are some excellent restaurants positioned to help you do so: **Robert et Compagnie** (p. 43) at the top of the street, **Restofiore** (p. 41) in the middle and **Boccacino's** (p. 46) at the southern end. For value, Restofiore cannot be beaten – and the on-the-street ambiance is free (or at least included).

Old Montreal

Old Montreal is also a great venue for terrasses. Place Jacques Cartier boasts the largest number in Old Montreal. The ground floor properties of the entire square are dedicated to terrasse eating. These places are always filled with tourists and serve accessible fare of all kinds. Service is competent to very good and the staff is generally friendly and eager to dispense advice on what to see and where to go in the city. **Le Jardin Nelson** (p. 41) is one of the busiest terrasses in Old Montreal, feeding thousands of tourists every year. Its inner terrasse is an impressive courtyard. Old Montreal is rampant with eye candy: heritage buildings, horse drawn *calèches*, cobblestone streets and tons of pedestrian traffic. West of St. Laurent/St. Lawrence Boulevard, the tourist traffic dies down and one can find a nice little spot to sit while taking in Old Montreal's Old World beauty. Whether you are looking for a place to eat, or a place to eat ice cream after eating, this is a great place to stroll.

Terrasse Fare

FOOD

Virtually any restaurant that has the ability to put tables outside will do so. As a result, the food served on terrasses ranges from adequate to excellent and everything from burgers, brunch, Chinese, French, Portuguese to Tibetan can be enjoyed outside in Montreal.

Regardless, terrasses are for summer eating. The food of summer is, or should be, light, refreshing and simple. If you're out on a terrasse avoid heavy, cream-laden food. Stick to the simple menu items and eat with the season. Enjoy cold soups such as *vichyssoise*, a cold potato and leek soup; or even *gazpacho*, the ultimate cold summer soup, a refreshing mix of tomatoes, cucumbers and bell peppers, spiked with sherry vinegar. Favour fresh salads, fish and seafood over heavy meats when enjoying a meal outdoors.

Atmosphere and ambiance are key to enjoying any meal, but it is especially true of terrasse dining. Become well-versed in the art of lingering. The reason it is sometimes so difficult to find a table on a terrasse is the expert lingering practised by most patrons of terrasses. Many can stretch a brunch, lunch or dinner into a languid and thoroughly enjoyable three hours. On many occasions, patrons enjoy a late lunch and stay on for a nice dinner under the stars.

If you find yourself on one of Montreal's many terrasses, we recommend that you enjoy one of the incredible micro-brewed beers that can be found on almost every terrasse on our little island. Montreal's microbreweries are among the world's most decorated. Enjoy a pint of Belle Gueule, Griffon Extra Pale Ale or St. Ambroise. If you have an urge to 'go foreign', we recommend Stella Artois or Harp. Beer, much like food, always tastes better with sun on your face.

'TERRASSE' WINE

Montreal wine drinkers tend to drink by season. The summer craze here belongs to rosé. (By the way, rosé should not be forgotten over the winter, as it matches the spicy and sweet dishes found on all kinds of Montreal menus.) The higher the alcohol level on the bottle, the drier, bolder and darker the wine will be in your glass – so be sure to check. You can rest assured that, except for White Zinfandel from California, most rosés are fermented dry and have an overall flavouring to match their colour. Most of what is available at the SAQ is imported from the south of France, but there are great finds from the Italians as well. Tavel is the quintessential rosé, but can be bitter, so unless you like that style, you may want to stick with the Pays d'Ôc region.

Australians have sparkling Shiraz and Italians offer Lambrusco. These wines are extra special as they are red and sparkling, a nice play on rosé.

Other recommended summer wines include Canadian Chardonnay and Pinot Blanc from Niagara or the Okanogan. The value is outstanding and the wine in the bottle generally surprises the average drinker.

When choosing a red wine, lean towards the lighter bodies,

like Beaujolais. Having lost its appeal in the 1980's, this wine region is seeing a revival.

Better selections from each region are making their way to SAQ shelves and should not be missed. Pick up a region-specific wine like Juliénas or Moulin à Vent and you can match lighter summer-based dishes to your drink. *Gamay*-based wines hold up to light and creamy sauces, as well as to medium-flavoured cheeses.

Best Terrasses

· Best terrasse for breakfast: **Café Cherrier** (p. 40) and **La Petite Ardoise** (p. 136)
· Most romantic: **Il Cortile** (p. 47)
· Best bar terrasse: **Tokyo Bar** (p. 160) (rooftop terrasse) and **St-Sulpice** (p. 157)
· Best hidden gem: **Café Santropol** (p. 40)
· Most luxurious: **Bice** (p. 45) and the **Ritz Garden** (p. 43)
· Best for burgers and beer: **Claremont** (p. 45)
· Tourist mecca: **Le Jardin Nelson** (p. 41)

◎ *Bistro*

ALEXANDRE

1454 Peel Area, Downtown
(514) 288-5105 $30 to $45
Refined cuisine. Specialties:
sauerkraut, veal liver and confit
of duck. Effervescent ambiance.
Brunches.

BORIS BISTRO

465 McGill, Old Montreal
(514) 848-9575   *$15 to $30*
Bistro which has won several
Montreal 'Design Commerce'
contests for its decor. Specialty:
crystallized duck. Large terrasse.

CAFÉ CHERRIER

3635 St. Denis, Plateau
(514) 843-4308
Bistro with a very quaint decor.
Ideal for breakfasts.

GRILL BISTRO 1 (LE)

183 St. Paul East,
Old Montreal
(514) 397-1044   *$15 to $30*
Fine French cuisine. The quality
of service creates the ambiance.
Table d'hôte every day with
specials for lunch. Beautiful
terrasse.

JAMES ROOSTER ESQ.

3 de la Commune,
Old Montreal
(514) 842-3822   *$15 to $30*
Pub and sports bar. Ambiance is
18th and 19th century, which,
given its history as John McGill's
trading house, makes sense.

Menu items include chicken and
ribs, appetizers and upmarket
sandwiches. Terrasse in the
summer.

PARIS-BEURRE (LE)

1226 Van Horne, Mount Royal
(514) 271-7502   *$15 to $30*
Casual Parisian bistro. Specialties:
veal sweetbreads, sirloin steak
and crème brûlée. Lunch and
dinner table d'hôte. Splendid
terrasse with garden.

ROSALIE

1232 Mountain (de la
Montagne), Downtown
(514) 392-1970   *$15 to $30*
Trendy French bistro. A touch of
St. Laurent on Mountain St. A
variety of main dishes, including
duck, tuna and rabbit. Large
terrasse in front.

◎ *Café*

CAFÉ DES ECLUSIERS

Parc des Ecluses,
Old Montreal
(514) 496-9767   *$15 to $30*
Open café located in Old
Montreal. Considered by locals to
be one of the best 'cinq à sept'
happy hour hotspots of the city.
Large terrasse.

CAFÉ SANTROPOL

3990 St. Urbain, Plateau
(514) 842-3110   *Under $15*
Cafe specialized in soups and
sandwiches (fresh style cheese).
Large terrace and garden.

Coloured decor. Ambiance:
Cordial and without pretension.

COTÉ SOLEIL

3979 St. Denis, Plateau
(514) 282-8037   *$15 to $30*
Specialties: grilled sirloin steak,
mussels and rack of lamb. Cordial
ambiance. Two terrasses during
the summer. Diversified wine list.

RESTOFIORE

705 St. Catherine St. West
(entrance on McGill College),
Downtown
(514) 288-7777
Typically Italian and French
cuisine. Perfect for business
people and for sports nights.
Relaxed environment. Separate
bar and nonsmoking section.
Table d'hôte offered during
dinner includes an entrée, salad,
main dish and mussels.

⊚ Creperie

JARDIN NELSON (LE)

407 Pl. Jacques Cartier,
Old Montreal
(514) 861-5731   *$15 to $30*
Pancake restaurant located in the
heart of the Old Montreal. Menu
composed of crêpes, pizzas,
salads, etc. Casual ambiance and,
depending on the weather, live
music (classical music or jazz).
Large terrasse. Open for over
25 years.

⊚ Dance Club

NEWTOWN

1476 Crescent, Downtown
(514) 284-6555
Fabulous restaurant owned by
none other than Jacques
Villeneuve himself. Renowned
and chic establishment, four
floors, terrasse, lounge and
discotheque. European ambiance.
Table d'hôte offered during lunch
and dinner (changed every two
weeks).

⊚ Fast Food

L'APARTÉ

5029 St. Denis, Plateau
(514) 282-0911   *$15 to $30*
A wide variety of coffee brands.
Fast service at an affordable
price: couscous, sandwiches and
grilled meats. Small terrasse.

⊚ Fondue

LAVAL & NORTH SHORE

JARDIN DES FONDUES

186 St. Marie, Terrebonne
(450) 492-2048   *$15 to $30*
Fine cuisine. Restaurant
specializes in fondues. Capacity
of 65. Table d'hôte offered every
evening. Romantic ambiance with
a terrasse during the summer.

@ *French*

ISLAND OF MONTREAL

BISTRO GOURMET 2 (AU)

4007 St. Denis, Plateau
(514) 844-0555   *$15 to $30*
French specialties with a
diversified menu. Dishes
presented with style. Try the
roasted sirloin steak and the
lamb. Traditional decor with a
bistro ambiance. Terrasse that
seats 25 is open in the summer.
Pleasant service.

DALI MATISSE

900 Duluth East, Plateau
(514) 845-6557   *$15 to $30*
Bring your own wine. French and
international cuisine. Try their
game meat triad (stag, pheasant,
ostrich), the skate and paella of
Valencia. Seats 50. Terrasse of 20
places open in the summer.
Cordial decor; bistro ambiance.

DEUX GAULOISES (AUX)

5195 Côte des Neiges,
Mount Royal
(514) 733-6867   *$15 to $30*
Seafood restaurant that offers
Breton crêpes. Special of the day
offered during lunch and a table
d'hôte for dinner. Capacity of 50
clients. Cordial and family
oriented ambiance. Large
terrasse. Open for over 20 years.

IMPRÉVU (L')

163 St. Jacques,
St. Jean sur Richelieu
(450) 346-2417   *$15 to $30*
Fine French cuisine with a varied
menu: seafood, offals and
prepared dishes. Casual
ambiance. Capacity of 100 with a
terrasse of 60 seats.

LEBLANC

3435 St. Laurent Blvd.
(St. Lawrence), Plateau
(514) 288-9909   *$30 to $45*
International fusion-style cuisine.
Several dishes influenced by
Italian, Californian and French
gastronomy. Special of the day.
Lounge ambiance with rhythm
and blues musicians every day.
Small terrasse open in the
summer.

MAISON PIERRE DU CALVET

405 Bonsecours,
Old Montreal
(514) 282-1725   *$30 to $45*
Fine cuisine with a varied menu
which includes game meats.
Romantic ambiance with an
interior terrasse, a Victorian room
with parrots, a dining room with
a foyer, a balcony on the second
floor and a VIP room with a
library.

MICHAEL W.

2601 Centre, South End
(514) 931-0821   *$15 to $30*
Franco-Italian restaurant
specializing in game meats. Try
their pears with blue, the ceviche

and their crème brûlée. Beautiful terrasse. Four dining rooms with a total capacity of 75 clients. Pleasant and intimate ambiance. Bring your own wine.

PEN CASTEL

1224 Ranger, North End
(514) 331-4945 $15 to $30
French restaurant specializing in game meats. Cordial and intimate ambiance. Small restaurant of 35 places. Table d'hôte served during lunch and dinner. Flowered terrasse. Large parking lot.

REMPARTS (LES)

93 de la Commune East, Old Montreal
(514) 392-1649 $30 to $45
Fine cuisine. Rather romantic and calm ambiance with a historical decor. Table d'hôte is only offered during lunch. Terrasse on the sixth floor with a view of the St. Lawrence River.

RESTO GUY ET DODO MORALI

1444 Metcalfe, Downtown
(514) 842-3636 $15 to $30
Fine restaurant specializing in confit of duck. Welcoming ambiance with a private room for 18 people. Table d'hôte offered during lunch and dinner; 114 wines. Internal and external terrasse. Indoor parking. Open for over 25 years.

RITZ GARDEN (THE)

1228 Sherbrooke St. West, Downtown
(514) 842-4212 $30 to $45
Elegant restaurant located in the Ritz-Carlton hotel. French gastronomy. Several specialties. The garden (with a pond and terrasse) is open during the summer. Chic and refined ambiance: pianist and artist on occasion. Several reception rooms are available.

ROBERT ET COMPAGNIE

2095 McGill College, Downtown
(514) 849-2742 $15 to $30
Chic bistro offering a cordial ambiance and decorated like a cathedral. Varied menu, composed of traditional dishes: tilapia, confit of duck and salads.

ROTONDE (LA)

185 St. Catherine St. West, Downtown
(514) 847-6900 $15 to $30
Cuisine of Provence. Specialties: 'encornet à la sétoise', duck breast glazed in honey and lavender and shepherd-style rack of lamb. Good selection of desserts. Beautiful and large terrasse.

LAVAL & NORTH SHORE

FOLICHON (LE)

804 St. François Xavier, Terrebonne
(450) 492-1863   *$15 to $30*
Restaurant located in a house dating from the 19th century. Diversified menu: rognons, duck liver, seafood, etc. Cordial and quiet ambiance with a foyer. On two floors with a 70 seat terrasse.

SOUTH SHORE

CÔTE à CÔTE (LE)

12 St. Mathieu, Beloeil
(450) 464-1633   *$15 to $30*
Restaurant specializing in grilled meats and seafood. Cordial and intimate ambiance. Specials available occasionally. Capacity of 60 clients with a large terrasse of about a hundred places.

JOZÉPHIL (LE)

969 Richelieu, Beloeil
(450) 446-9751   *$15 to $30*
Fine French cuisine. Table d'hôte offered during lunch and dinner. Intimate and rustic ambiance and decor. Beautiful terrasse with a view of the Richelieu and Mont St. Hilaire. Capacity of 45.

MAISON BLEUE (LA)

2592 Bourgogne, Montérégie
(450) 447-1112   *$15 to $30*
House dating back to 1815. Specialties: game meats, seafood and a great selection of offals. Large open and closed terrasse

under a top. Reception room. Calm ambiance. Brunch on Sundays. Children under six eat for free.

◎ *German*

BERLIN

101 Fairmount West, Plateau
(514) 270-3000
Authentic German cuisine. Beautiful ambiance during the week; beer garden atmosphere on weekends. Table d'hôte from Sunday to Thursday. Musicians on occasions. Seats 85.

◎ *Greek*

JARDIN DE PUITS

180 Villeneuve East, Plateau
(514) 849-0555   *$15 to $30*
Quality menu at a reasonable price. Summer terrasse with a capacity of 120 people. Cordial ambiance.

PSAROTAVERNA DU SYMPOSIUM

3829 St. Denis, Plateau
(514) 842-0867   *$15 to $30*
Specialized in cuisine from the Greek islands. Large variety of fresh fish and seafood. Terrasse for 20 people in the summer.

PSAROTAVERNA DU SYMPOSIUM

5334 Park Ave, Plateau
(514) 274-7022   *$15 to $30*

⊚ Indian

SHED TANDOORI
4886A Sources Blvd.,
West Island
(514) 683-8737 *$15 to $30*
Authentic cuisine at an affordable
price. Menu à la carte and table
d'hôte offered for lunch and
dinner. Famous restaurant for its
fine cuisine and its decor.
Capacity of 50 clients with a
terrasse.

⊚ International

CÉPAGE (AU)
212 Notre Dame West,
Old Montreal
(514) 845-5436 *$15 to $30*
Contemporary bistro with a
diversified menu: French, Italian,
Indian, Spanish, etc, cuisine.
Personalized menu. Beautiful
ambiance with a bar and a
terrasse. Several rooms. Ideal for
parties.

CLAREMONT
5032 Sherbrooke St. West,
West End
(514) 483-1557
Restaurant with a casual and
relaxed style - not too chic. A
large variety of international
dishes. Try their calamari and
their dumplings.

TERRASSE LAFAYETTE
250 Villeneuve West, Plateau
(514) 288-3915 *$15 to $30*
Cordial ambiance with a summer
terrasse. Large variety: French,

Canadian, Italian and Greek
cuisine. Buy three small pizzas
and the fourth one is free. Bring
your own wine.

⊚ Irish

HURLEY'S
1225 Crescent, Downtown
(514) 861-4111 *$15 to $30*
Restaurant-bar with terrasse,
specializing in imported beers.
Animated and cordial place;
typical Irish ambiance.

MCKIBBIN'S
1426 Bishop, Downtown
(514) 288-1580 *$15 to $30*
Great establishment of three
floors with a pub, restaurant and
discotheque. Menu à la carte with
a happy hour from 5 pm to 8 pm,
Monday to Friday. Musicians
every day. Quiz night on Mondays
with prizes to be won. Irish
ambiance.

⊚ Italian

ISLAND OF MONTREAL

BICE
1504 Sherbrooke St. West,
Downtown
(514) 937-6009 *$30 to $45*
Four star restaurant of fine Italian
cuisine. Good choice of
traditional Italian dishes and
seafood. Good wine list. Elegant
and smart ambiance. Two floors
able to seat 100.

BOCCACINO'S RESTAURANT

1253 McGill College,
Downtown
(514) 861-5742   under $15
Italian cuisine with a varied menu.
Great selection of entrées, soups,
salads, sandwiches, pastas, pizzas
and international dishes. Copious
breakfasts. Beautiful environment
adapted to all occasions. Table
d'hôte during the evening.

D'AMICHI

25 Blvd. Bishop Power,
South End
(514) 595-9199 $15 to $30
Family restaurant that has won
several awards. Splendid view of
the rapids and large open
terrasse in the summer. Varied
menu: pasta, seafood, meats.
Table d'hôte offered all week.

DA MARCELLO

1251 Gilford, Plateau
(514) 524-3812 $15 to $30
Fine Tuscan cuisine. Romantic
ambiance with a summer
terrasse. Table d'hôte changes
each day. Sampling menu and
menu à la carte include
homemade pasta and seafood.
Reception room.

DIVA (LA)

1273 Blvd. René Lévesque
(fka Dorchester) East,
East End
(514) 523-3470 $15 to $30
Small Italian restaurant with a
terrasse. Authentic and sublime
cuisine. Fresh ingredients

prepared with meticulousness.
Table d'hôte offered during lunch
and dinner. Large variety of
dishes; specialty of the house:
veal liver with onions.

FERRARI

1407 Bishop, Downtown
(514) 843-3086 $15 to $30
Restaurant-bistro with a cordial
ambiance, perfect for business
people. Specialty: homemade
pasta. Table d'hôte offered during
lunch and dinner. Large terrasse
during the summer.

FOCCACIA DI CARPACCIO

2077 University, Downtown
(514) 284-1115 $15 to $30
Fine restaurant specializing in
homemade pasta. Menu à la carte
and buffet from 5 pm to 7 pm.
Restaurant-bar ambiance with a
terrasse and from time to time,
live music.

IL BOCCALINI

1408 de l'Église, North End
(514) 747-7809 $15 to $30
Fine Italian and Mediterranean
cuisine. Very elegant
Mediterranean decor. Beautiful
open terrasse during the summer.
Specialties: Italian and
Mediterranean swordfish. Menu
includes grilled meats, veal,
pastas, pizzas and seafood. Table
d'hôte every evening starting at
$23.

IL CORTILE
42 Sherbrooke St. West,
Downtown
(514) 843-8230 *$30 to $45*
Description: The menu includes a
variety of traditional dishes which
change according to the seasons.
Choice of pastas, meats and
refined fish. Good selection of
Italian wines. It is preferable to
reserve on the weekend.

IL FORNETTO
1900 St. Joseph, West Island
(514) 637-5253   *$15 to $30*
Large restaurant of fine Italian
cuisine specializing in pasta,
pizzas and seafood. Table d'hôte
offered during lunch and dinner.
Terrasse is situated right next to
the St. Louis canal. Very cordial.

MARCO
82 St. Anne, West Island
(514) 457-3850   *$15 to $30*
Large Italian and Greek restaurant
specializing in pizzas and other
Mediterranean dishes. Table
d'hôte offered during lunch and
dinner includes coffee and soup.
Terrasse with a beautiful view of
the river.

NAPOLI
1675 St. Denis, Plateau
(514) 845-5905   *$15 to $30*
Home-style cuisine with a vast
choice of dishes: pasta, meats,
seafood. Rustic Italian ambiance.
Table d'hôte includes soup or
salad, entrée and a main dish.
Two terrasses during the summer.

PASTA ANDREA
1718 St. Joseph, West Island
(514) 634-3400   *$15 to $30*
Excellent Italian restaurant with a
remarkable value for the money.
Refined cuisine with a table
d'hôte offered during lunch and
dinner which includes several
choices of entrées, main dishes
and desserts. Terrasse with a
beautiful view of the Lachine
canal.

PASTA TELLA
2055 Stanley, Downtown
(514) 842-5344   *$15 to $30*
Italian and Swiss restaurant,
specializing in fresh pastas and
fondues. Table d'hôte offered
during lunch and dinner. Capacity
of 140 with a private room of 40
places and a terrasse.

PICOLLA ITALIA
6701 St. Laurent Blvd. (St.
Lawrence), Mount Royal
(514) 270-6701   *$30 to $45*
Italian restaurant, small summer
terrasse. Elegant decor, diligent
service. Excellent wine list. A lot
of spirit and Italian music.

RESTAURANT D'AVERSA
700 de la Gauchetière West,
Downtown
(514) 874-9959   *$30 to $45*
Fine Italian cuisine. Romantic and
cordial ambiance. Eight tables
d'hôtes with five dishes. Menu à
la carte every day. Happy hour
(5 pm to 7 pm), breakfast and

children's menu on Saturdays.
Terrasse with 80 places.

TAORMINA

2530 St. Joseph, West Island
(514) 634-5548   *$15 to $30*
Fine Italian cuisine. Romantic and
casual ambiance. Specialties:
seafood, homemade pasta and
veal. Reception room, two
terrasses and free parking.

TARANTELLA (LA)

184 Jean Talon East,
Mount Royal
(514) 278-3067   *$15 to $30*
Fine Italian cuisine. Restaurant
with a terrasse on the Jean Talon
market side and a bistro section.
Traditional and modern dishes.
Fresh pasta.

TRATTORIA CAPRICCIOSA

5220 Decarie Blvd.,
Mount Royal
(514) 487-1234   *$15 to $30*
Small restaurant of fine cuisine.
Friendly, romantic and typical
Italian ambiance. Select wines.
Musician on Fridays and
Saturdays. Reception room,
terrasse and free parking.

VIA ROMA

7064 St. Laurent Blvd.
(St. Lawrence), Mount Royal
(514) 277-3301   *$15 to $30*
Typical Italian cuisine and
ambiance. Varied menu:
homemade pasta, seafood, fish,
pizzas. Table d'hôte is only served
during lunch and includes an

entrée, main dish and coffee.
External terrasse open year long.

VIEUX FOUR MANAGO (LE)

3636 Blvd. St. Charles,
West Island
(514) 428-0100   *$15 to $30*
Restaurant specializing in pizzas
cooked in a wood oven. Cordial
ambiance around the oven. Table
d'hôte offered during the
evening. Terrasse with 60 places
open during the summer.

LAVAL & NORTH SHORE

PALMO

533 Principale, Laval
(450) 689-4141   *$15 to $30*
Pleasant restaurant, ideal for
romantic or family evenings.
Establishment with a foyer and a
terrasse. Large variety of dishes:
seafood, veal, game meats,
grilled meats. Reception room for
big groups.

VIEUX FOUR (AU)

300 Sicard, Laval
(450) 437-4100   *$15 to $30*
Magnificent restaurant that has a
stone floor and a wooden roof.
Pizza cooked in a wood oven.
Good pasta, steak, veal and
chicken. Café that offers an
amazing happy hour (5 pm to 7
pm) every evening, Monday
through Friday. Large terrasse
during the summer.

SOUTH SHORE

LUIGGI

3271 Taschereau Blvd. East,
Greenfield Park
(450) 671-1617   *$15 to $30*
Restaurant with two sections.
Specialties: pastas, filet mignon,
seafood. A different table d'hôte
every day. Cordial and casual
ambiance. Breakfast served every
day (served on a terrasse during
weekends).

RISTORANTE LA BARCA

540 rte. Marie-Victorin,
Boucherville
(450) 641-2277   *$15 to $30*
Fine typical Italian cuisine.
Specialties: seafood, pastas and
pizzas cooked in a wood oven.
Homemade pastas and desserts.
Cordial, romantic and family
ambiance. Reception room with a
capacity from 20 to 80 people.
Terrasse and pergola during
the summer.

TAVOLA (LA)

352 Guillaume, Longueuil
(450) 928-1433   *$15 to $30*
Small local restaurant with a
cordial ambiance. Splendid
European-style terrasse.
Specialties: homemade smoked
salmon and fresh pastas.

TRATTORIA LA TERRAZZA

575 Victoria, St. Lambert
(450) 672-7422   *$15 to $30*
Classic Italian restaurant. Typical
home-style cuisine. Specialties:

homemade pasta, seafood and
veal. Capacity of 80 clients and
70 on the terrasse. Establishment
located in the downtown area.

◎ *Jazz*

UPSTAIRS JAZZ CLUB & RESTO

1254 Mackay, Downtown
(514) 931-6808
Menu with several specialties:
beefsteak of ribs, lamb, grilled
salmon, mahi mahi and calamari.
Elegant ambiance with a small
grand piano and an aquarium;
in short, ideal for couples.
Musicians playing every day
during the winter and from
Monday to Thursday during the
summer. Excellent wine list.

◎ *Japanese*

ISLAND OF MONTREAL

ATAMI

5499 Côte des Neiges,
Mount Royal
(514) 735-5400   *$15 to $30*
Small cordial restaurant, with a
sushi counter. Large terrasse with
a capacity from 30 to 40 people
during the summer. Table d'hôte
offered during lunch and dinner
includes an entrée, salad, main
dish, dessert and tea. $5 fee for
any delivery.

SOUTH SHORE

SHOGUN (1983)
6155 Taschereau Blvd.,
Brossard
(450) 678-3868   *$15 to $30*
Restaurant of fine Japanese
cuisine with a sushi counter and
heated tables. Semi-modern
ambiance. Table d'hôte offered
every day. Tatami room and
summer terrasse.

◎ *Lebanese/Syrian*

ALEP
199 Jean Talon East, Mount
Royal
(514) 270-6396   *$15 to $30*
Restaurant of fine cuisine, bistro
and terrasse. Typical Syrian
ambiance. Menu à la carte only.

SAMIRAMISS
885 Decarie Blvd., North End
(514) 747-3085   *$15 to $30*
Lebanese home-style cooking.
Family ambiance and cordial
environment. Summer terrasse.
Specialties: grilled Lebanese
meats and seafood. Specials and
menu à la carte are offered
every day.

◎ *Mediterranean*

NEWTOWN
1476 Crescent, Downtown
(514) 284-6555   *$30 to $45*
Fabulous restaurant owned by
none other than Jacques
Villeneuve himself. Renowned
and chic establishment with four
floors, a terrasse, a lounge and
discotheque. European ambiance.
Table d'hôte offered during lunch
and dinner (changed every two
weeks).

◎ *Mexican*

EL MESON
1678 Blvd. St. Joseph,
West Island
(514) 634-0442   *$15 to $30*
Traditional Mexican home-style
cooking. Authentic ambiance, two
terrasses. Table d'hôte offered
during lunch from 11 am to 3 pm.
Menu à la carte also offered.

◎ *Pizzeria*

PIZZAFIORE
3518 Lacombe, Mount Royal
(514) 735-1555   *$15 to $30*
Cordial ambiance, visible wood
oven and rustic decor. Several
specials. Capacity of 70 clients
with a reception room. Three
terrasses, one European in style.

◎ *Portuguese*

SOLMAR
111 St. Paul East,
Old Montreal
(514) 861-4562   *$15 to $30*
Fine Portuguese cuisine.
Specialties: seafood and grilled
meats. Menu includes a three-
dish special starting at $40,
which includes an entrée, soup,
salad, main dish, dessert and
coffee. Portuguese ambiance.
Terrasse on the first floor.

⑥ *Québécois*

CABARET DU ROY (LE)

363 de la Commune E.,
Old Montreal
(514) 907-9000   *$30 to $45*
Thematic restaurant with actors
and musicians acting out 18th
century parts. Table d'hôte
includes two entrées, main dish,
dessert and coffee. Special menu
for groups of 20 and above.
Two terrasses.

⑥ *Resto-Bar*

AVENTURE

438 Pl. Jacques Cartier, Old
Montreal
(514) 866-9439   *$15 to $30*
French and Italian cuisine.
European and modern decor.
Two floors, capacity of 280
clients and two terrasses.

RESTAURANT CUBE

355 McGill, Old Montreal
(514) 876-2823
Located in Hotel St. Paul, this is a
'place-to-be-seen' in Old
Montreal. Always stylish without
sacrificing the quality of its food,
Restaurant Cube prides itself in
presenting the best Canada has
to offer: salmon from New
Brunswick, lamb from Alberta,
veal from Quebec, etc. The wine
list is primarily French with
notable exceptions, lunch is only
$23 for three courses.

OLDE ORCHARD
PUB & GRILL

5563 Monkland, West End
(514) 484-1569
The Olde Orchard is a
neighbourhood pub. We'd like to
say 'typical', but they are not
common! Great pub atmosphere,
excellent pub food and good
selection of beers. Live Celtic
music on some nights. The crow
is a mix of ages and walks of life.
Large room at the back. Terrasse
in front.

PETITE ARDOISE (LA)

222 Laurier West, Plateau
(514) 495-4961
French cuisine that offers a table
d'hôte during lunch and dinner.
Parisian ambiance and decor, with
garden.

⑥ *Seafood*

DELFINO

1231 Lajoie, Mount Royal
(514) 277-5888   *$30 to $45*
Restaurant specializing in fresh
fish and seafood. Popular place.
Table d'hôte includes three
dishes. Large, open terrasse
during summer.

MOULERIE (LA)

1249 Bernard West,
Mount Royal
(514) 273-8132   *$15 to $30*
Restaurant specializing in
mussels. Bistro-style. Friendly
ambiance. Large terrasse of 105
places. Well situated
establishment.

@ *Spanish*

CASA GALICIA (LA)

2087 St. Denis, Downtown
(514) 843-6698   *$15 to $30*
Typical Spanish ambiance.
Specialties: paellas and various
seafood plates. Flamenco show
with musicians Fridays and
Saturdays. Table d'hôte during
lunch and dinner. Terrasse in the
summer.

DONA MARIA

520 Beaubien East, Plateau
(514) 272-5885
Latino food at bargain prices.
Specializing in dishes from El
Salvador, nothing on the menu
costs more than $16. Features a
relaxed atmosphere, quick
service and good-sized portions.
Open for both lunch and dinner,
their guacamole, enchiladas and
cold soups are always a safe bet.

@ *Swiss*

CHEZ TRUDI

445 Lakeshore (Bord du Lac),
West Island
(514) 631-1403   *$15 to $30*
Fine European cuisine. Specialty:
fondues. Rustic and cordial
ambiance similar to a country
cottage. Excellent quality/price
value. Summer terrasse.

RACLETTE (LA)

1059 Gilford, Plateau
(514) 524-8118   *$15 to $30*
Swiss and European style cuisine.
Specialties: fondue and raclette.
Large variety of European dishes:

duck, scallops, filet mignon, etc.
Small and big table d'hôte,
private room and a summer
terrasse. Bring your own wine.

@ *Thai*

THAI-VIET

3610 St. Dominique, Plateau
(514) 288-5577   *$15 to $30*
Fine Vietnamese and Thai cuisine.
Diversified menu includes soups,
grilled meats, noodles and other
dishes. Terrasse with a capacity
of 80 people open during the
summer. Typical Asian decor.
Bring your own wine.

@ *Vietnamese*

ESCALE à SAIGON

107 Laurier West, Plateau
(514) 272-3456   *$15 to $30*
Fine Vietnamese cuisine. Plush
and elegant ambiance. Great
selection of authentic Vietnamese
dishes served with an artistic
flair. Lunch specials and table
d'hôte include an entrée, main
dish with perfumed rice and a
dessert. Terrasse with a capacity
of 20 people.

SOUVENIRS D'INDOCHINE

243 Mount Royal W., Plateau
(514) 848-0336   *$15 to $30*
Fine cuisine, highly regarded for
over 10 years. Varied menu:
noodles, sautéed dishes, seafood,
rolls, soups. Zen ambiance.
Artistic clientele during the week
and a more family clientele on
weekends. Art exposition on
occasion. Terrasse with view of
the mountain.

Chapter 3.
Reasonable Dining ($15 to $30)

Due to the sheer volume of reasonably priced restaurants, this guide would become biblical in size if every genre and sub-genre were covered and reviewed. Reasonable dining is day-to-day eating, which should comprise simple, well-prepared and affordably priced food.

This section will discuss some of the culinary offerings in Montreal and the most popular dishes offered at each, how to identify what's well prepared and what to expect from specific culinary styles.

French – Spotlight on the Bistro

Food

For obvious reasons, French food is a large part of Montreal's culinary landscape and it is done exceptionally well. Much like the Italians, the French focus on simplicity and the best ingredients. There are differences, though. The Italians are passionate about their food, but treat it with a loose, casual style. The French possess an exceptional love of cooking: their passion is so deep that they apply an almost scientific approach to building each dish. In French cooking, the details are painstakingly monitored, the ingredients pored over and recipes are followed with exactitude. Perfection is striven for in every dish, however simple.

Bordelaise sauce is a staple in French cuisine. It generally accompanies grilled meats, most usually a rare filet mignon. *Bordelaise* is prepared over several days. Veal and beef bones are roasted for several hours and the juice is saved. It is added to a stockpot with a *bouquet garni* (herbs and vegetables wrapped in cheese cloth), onion, garlic, carrot, leek and water. As red wine is added and the stock simmers, the sauce is continually monitored, skimmed and put through a series of strainers, until it is reduced from several liters to a few cups of rich sauce infused with essence of beef. This sauce complements a cooked piece of beef perfectly, but takes days to make. That is the essence of French cuisine: technically difficult, precisely executed – a mixture of passion and rigid patience.

The bistro is the most immediate and gratifying way to enjoy French cuisine, and Montreal is rife with them. The bulk of bistro menus generally offer the same set of dishes. Their execution defines the quality of the establishment.

◎ *Steak frites*. The French interpretation of meat and potatoes. The *steak frites* is the definitive bistro meal: sirloin steak grilled to perfection, topped with a knob of garlic butter and accompanied with perfectly crisped French fries. The French fries are usually twice fried to achieve crispiness on the inside of the fry and a golden color on the outside. The *frites* are always served with mayonnaise (often spiked with garlic, lemon juice and parsley).

◎ *Confit de canard*. This dish is another perfect expression of the patience of French cuisine. A duck leg is cooked in its own fat for several hours, then packed in the same fat and stored for at least a month. When ready to serve, the leg is retrieved from its congealed carapace, heated and served atop a mound of lightly dressed salad greens. The meat falls beautifully off the bone.

◎ *Steak tartare*. Another exceptional example of bistro fare. Raw filet mignon (traditionally horse meat) is hand cut and mixed with a variety of ingredients, most typically minced red onion, capers, parsley, Tabasco sauce, Worcestershire sauce, Dijon mustard and egg yolks. Steak Tartare is always accompanied with toasted bread and *frites*.

◎ *Onion Soup*. A bistro classic. Rich onion soup topped with crusty slices of baguette and gruyere cheese. An ideal soup to enjoy during the winter months.

◎ *Moules marinière*. Mussels steamed in garlic, shallots, white wine and tomatoes (or tomato sauce) served, as always, with *frites*.

◎ *Cassoulet à l'ancienne*. A typical dish from the south of France, with duck confit, lamb and Toulouse sausage served with white beans, tomatoes, pork rashers and rosemary. This dish epitomizes Provençal cooking.

◎ *Crème brulée*. Literally translated, 'burnt cream'. It is on every bistro dessert menu and is absolutely delicious. It is comprised of a vanilla-infused custard, topped with sugar, which is then caramelized, forming a crispy-sugary outer layer, which hides the cold custard within. It is very rich.

WINE FOR FRENCH FOOD

French food and French wine go hand in hand, but when choosing a wine for your enjoyment, the question is whether to experiment or stick with an old stand-by.

Start the evening cleansing the palate with a Spanish or Californian bubbly, move onto Chilean Chardonnay bursting with tropical fruit and citrus flavours and then hit the reds with gusto. Establishments like **Bistro Gourmet 2** (p. 84) have a menu well suited to Bordeaux blends filled with the black fruit flavours of Cabernet Sauvignon and chocolate and plum overtones from Merlot. Select a mid-priced Bordeaux or a higher priced, premium California Cabernet-based wine for these types of menus. French food can stand up to Australian Shiraz and some good *Chianti* or *Barbaresco* with their bolder flavours being tamed by the cream-based sauces and cheese selections.

If you want to splurge, have a good Burgundy from Mercury with steak tartare. The freshness of the meat's flavour will pair delicately with the earthiness of the wine.

GREAT MONTREAL BISTROS
- **L'Entrecôte St-Jean** (p. 69)
- **Steak Frites St-Paul** (p. 71-2)
- **Continental** (p. 69)
- **Café Cherrier** (p. 68)
- **Au Petit Extra** (p. 71)

Spanish

Recently, the most excitement and attention in the culinary world has been given to the food and chefs of Spain. All the current food trends, adopted by chefs the world over, were born in the minds of Spanish chefs. Spain has a history of many different cultural influences contributing to the richness and variety of its cuisine. Spanish cuisine has become so popular because of its sense of fun. Spaniards have an incredible balance of love, respect and intense creativity when it comes to the preparation of food. That sense of heart can always be felt when enjoying Spanish food. Traditional Spanish ingredients are: shrimp, chili peppers, *serrano* ham, shellfish (*mariscos*), anchovies, *chorizo* (a spicy sausage), beans, eggs, blood sausages, garlic, Spanish sherry, *baccalao* (dried salt cod), olives and olive oil.

Spanish food is best enjoyed in large groups. Even better, spend a long lazy night eating Spanish food and drinking with good friends well into the wee hours of the morning. In Spain, an early dinner starts at around 10:30 pm. The restaurants are usually packed around midnight. The Spanish restaurants in Montreal are generally quite authentic.

◉ *Tapas:* The most visible culinary contribution of Spain is *tapas* (snack-like finger food). *Tapas* bars are found everywhere in Spain. Each *tapas* bar has its own special set of signature dishes.

◉ *Paellas* are colourful and festive rice dishes. A variety of veg-

etables, meats, poultry and seafood are combined in rice forti-
fied with heavy stock and saffron. The traditional *paella* is a
combination of chicken, *chorizo,* shrimp, mussels and vegetables. Variations include ingredients such as rabbit, snails and
various fishes.

◉ *Gazpacho*: a delicious and refreshing cold soup consisting of
tomatoes, cucumber, peppers, breadcrumbs, sherry, ice and
herbs, finished with a swirl of heavy Spanish olive oil. It is the
perfect summer soup.

◉ *Tortilla* is a traditional Spanish omelette cooked with potato
slices. Generally enjoyed as *tapas*.

◉ *Churros* are another traditional favourite that must be
enjoyed. The *churro* serves as the truest test of a good Spanish
chef. *Churros* are Spanish-style doughnuts. The dough is formed
into a fluffy, cigar-shape, cooked and dusted with sugar.
Authentically presented *churros* will be served with a rich mug
of toothsome hot chocolate – much, much thicker than the North
American variety.

Great Spanish food:
· **Casa Tapas** (p. 139)
· **Don Miguel** (p. 139)

Asian

JAPANESE
Much like the French, the Japanese are meticulous when it
comes to technique and detail. They have a respect for tradition,
ingredients and execution. Montreal boasts an abundance of
Japanese restaurants that feature sushi and other traditional
menu items, and sushi has become a part of our culinary fabric.
Quality varies and is dependent on the establishment. There are
many places in Montreal that offer cut-rate sushi. Beware: you
may be getting what you pay for.

◉ *Sushi* is the quintessential symbol of Japanese cuisine. Sushi chefs in Japan are incredibly well-trained. Students training to become sushi chefs must spend one year perfecting the art of sushi rice preparation. There are very specific methods for slicing and handling raw fish, rolling maki, cutting and dicing each ingredient to exact specifications. The vinegared rice is dabbed with *wasabi* (Japanese horseradish turned into a paste) and topped with a variety of raw fish and seafoods.

◉ *Teriyaki* is a way of Japanese cooking. The word '*teriyaki*' is a combination of two Japanese words: '*teri*' and '*yaki*'. *Teri* means 'luster' and *yaki* means 'grill' or 'broil'. To make a teriyaki dish, ingredients are broiled, roasted or grilled, after being marinated in, or basted by, teriyaki sauce. It's the teriyaki sauce that brings the shiny look (*teri*) to the ingredients. The sauce is generally made from a reduction of rice wine (sake) or sherry, soya, ginger and other seasonings.

◉ *Miso soup* is a traditional Japanese soup, which is comprised of seaweed, tofu pieces, shitake mushrooms and *miso*. *Miso* is a rich, salty condiment that characterizes the essence of Japanese cooking. A smooth paste, *miso* is made from soybeans and a grain such as rice, plus salt and a mold culture, all aged in cedar vats for one to three years.

◉ *Tempura* refers to classic Japanese deep fried batter-dipped seafood and vegetables. The batter is made of ice-cold water or soda, flour and egg yolks. Small, dry, bite-sized pieces of food are dipped in flour, then in batter and then quickly deep-fried.

◉ *Gyoza*: fried or steamed meat or seafood-filled dumplings traditionally served with a sauce made from soya, mirin (rice wine vinegar) and lemon juice.

◉ *Green tea ice cream* is traditional Japanese ice cream made from green tea powder.

Great Japanese food
- **Kashima** (p. 123)
- **Mikasa Sushi Bar** (p. 124)
- **Sakura Garden** (p. 125)
- **Sho-Dan** (p. 125)

CHINESE

China is a vast country with an abundance of culinary styles beyond the Cantonese and Szechwan traditions. For instance, northern China has a distinct Mongolian influence in its cooking style, characterized through the simplicity of 'fire pot' or 'hot pot' cooking, attributable to the nomadic tradition of single pot cooking. Each city also possesses its own style.

North Americans have a love affair with Chinese cuisine, but the ever-popular dishes we order off Chinese menus aren't as authentic as we might expect and they would be hard to find in China. Luckily, there are some exceptional Chinese restaurants in Montreal that offer authentic Chinese cuisine. If one is willing to move beyond the obvious dishes and yearn to discover real Chinese cuisine, follow one simple rule: step away from the General Tao's chicken. (General Tao's chicken is, without a doubt, the most popular Chinese dish in North America. It is a deep fried piece of chicken coated in a sweet glaze, generally enjoyed with rice. It is named after a famous and very successful 19th century Chinese general, Tso T'sung-T'ang. The invention of the dish is attributed to Chinese restaurants in New York and San Francisco.)

Many Chinese restaurants possess two menus. The menu for the generic Americanized Chinese food enthusiasts (aka: the Caucasian menu) and the authentic menu. Be adventurous and order off the authentic menu. The following dishes are a mixture of the popular and authentic.

◎ *Dim Sum* is not unlike a series of *hors d'oeuvres*, originally stemming from Cantonese custom of tea drinking (*yum cha*). It consists of feasting on an assortment of small delicacies such as dumplings, steamed dishes, egg custards and more. It is the Chinese version of Sunday brunch and a fun way to enjoy a wondrous facet of Chinese cuisine. *Dim Sum* is enjoyed in large groups and characterized by large round tables and waiters pushing steam carts filled with various *dim sum* items for the table to share.

◎ *Peking duck* is a very special and authentic Chinese dish. It is meticulously prepared. When traditionally made, air is pumped into the duck to separate the skin from the fat. It is then hung up to dry in the open air before being slow roasted, until crispy on the outside and succulent on the inside. It is usually served in slices with rice pancakes and Hoisin sauce (a soya-based paste).

◎ *Black bean sauce* is a delicious blend of fermented black soy beans, garlic and Chinese spices served with noodles, seafood, beef and fish.

Great Authentic Chinese

· **Le Caveau Szechwan** (p. 74)
· **La Maison Kam Fung** (p. 76)
· **La Maison VIP** (p. 76)
· **Fu Kam Wah** (p. 75)

THAI

Thai food is simple, fragrant and influenced heavily by Indian and Chinese traditions. A Thai meal has no courses and is always built around rice. Rice is the main course and the hot dishes (e.g. curries) are eaten by the Thai more as sauces than main dishes. Thai food is either stir fried or steamed, always cooked in a wok. The staple ingredients in Thai food are coconut milk, lemon grass, palm sugar, cilantro (coriander), galangal (a cousin of ginger), fish sauce (*nam pla*) and, of course, chile. Due to the simplicity of Thai cuisine, good Thai can be had anywhere in Montreal.

◎ *Curry (red, green, golden, panang).* Thai curries were heavily influenced by the Indian curry tradition, in which coconut milk is used to curb the spicy kick, and are a staple of Thai cuisine. Based on a paste comprised of different chilies, garlic, galangal, cut with coconut milk and served with fish, chicken, seafood or beef. Best enjoyed with sticky rice.

◎ *Tom Yum Soup* is a spicy soup with lemon grass, kaffir lime leaves, fish sauce, lime, pineapple, tomatoes and shrimp. Generally spicy and very delicious.

◎ *Pad (also Phad) Thai.* Pad Thai, eaten in Thailand as a snack or lunch, is a ubiquitous entrée in Thai restaurants in North America. It is a dish of rice noodles tossed with bean sprouts, egg and shrimp in a light sauce comprised of red curry paste, palm sugar, fish sauce, then garnished with peanuts, cilantro and lime.

◎ *Satay.* Beef, pork, or chicken satay is an appetizer the Thais have adopted from Indonesia. It is skewered meat served with a peanut sauce and a mix of pickled vegetables.

◎ *Som Dtam.* Green papaya salad is another exceptional dish very popular in Thailand, comprised of green papaya, tomatoes and dried shrimp, along with the standard Thai ingredients of fish sauce, lime juice and palm sugar.

◎ *Sticky Rice.* A Thai staple, sticky rice is comprised of sweet glutinous rice cooked in a straw container, then steamed.

Great Thai
- **Phayathai** (p. 145)
- **Chao Phraya** (p. 144)
- **Thaïlande** (p. 145)
- **Thai Grill** (p. 145)
- **Chu Chai** (p. 144)

VIETNAMESE

Exceptional Vietnamese cuisine can be found in Montreal. Along the main strip of Chinatown, *pho* joints are always packed with diners slurping away at fragrant bowls of this Vietnamese noodle soup. Vietnamese food was profoundly influenced by the French colonization of Vietnam. Many French traditions, such as *baguette* and pâtés, are embedded in the Vietnamese culinary psyche. The staple ingredients in Vietnamese cooking are similar to Thai: fish sauce (*nuoc nam*), lemon grass, shrimp, garlic, basil, star anise and mint. The best way to get a taste of authentic Vietnamese cooking is to hit one of the many *pho* places on St. Laurent Boulevard in Chinatown.

◎ *Pho bo* is a beef noodle soup and the national dish of Vietnam. It is comprised of a beef stock flavoured with ginger, star anise, cloves and other spices. Rice noodles are added and topped with raw, paper thin slices of beef, which cook from the heat of the stock. Added to this are bean sprouts, fragrant basil leaves, lime juice and chilies. It is the perfect soup and the best introduction to Vietnamese cuisine.

◎ *Spring rolls*: Shrimp, mint, rice noodles, coriander, lettuce and thinly sliced pork are wrapped in rice paper and served cold with fish or peanut sauce.

◎ *Vietnamese coffee*: Vietnam's own interpretation of *café au lait*. It is thick espresso served over ice with condensed milk. For any coffee enthusiast, Vietnamese coffee is an absolute must.

Best Vietnamese:
· **Pho Bang New York** (p. 147)

INDIAN

Indian food is as diverse as the country's languages, regions, culture and climate. Every major region of India has its own contribution to the country's culinary fabric. Aromatic spices are the foundation of Indian cuisine: coriander, cumin, fenugreek and curry, among many others. Montreal has a great number of Indian restaurants that provide a fantastic assortment of authentic Indian cuisine.

◉ *Chicken tikka*: Tender morsels of chicken marinated in yogurt and tandoori spice and cooked in a *tandoor*, or clay cooking pot. Chicken *tikka* is generally served with rice, salad and a yogurt sauce. *Naan* bread can accompany this dish.

◉ *Naan bread*: Indian flat bread cooked in a *tandoor* and served with *ghee*, a clarified butter. *Naan* is an incredibly delicious, sweet, soft bread served hot with char marks on it.

◉ *Samosa*: a fried turnover stuffed with a variety of ingredients, meat, potatoes and peas.

◉ *Bhajia*: strings of onion batter fried until reaching golden perfection.

Great Indian Food
· **Taj Mahal de l'Ouest** (p. 99)

WINE FOR ASIAN FOOD

Asian food, with its spicy or sour overtones, generally pairs better with a light tasting and sparkly beer. When wine is the accompaniment, choose a sake that is meant to be drunk cold, like Shobu. It comes in a frosted bottle to block the light. Most restos have the draft variety, which for a cheap drink is quite pleasant. It is appealing because it goes down the throat quite smoothly and has a slightly alcoholic aftertaste. But ordering draft of any kind may cheapen your meal. Cold sake will have an aftertaste of fragrant flowers and will have a thicker mouthfeel.

If European wine is the choice, then open a *Gewürztraminer* or *Riesling* from Alsace, Germany or even Canada. Their fragrant and slightly sweet taste can tame even the spiciest dish on the menu.

◎ *Afghan*

CAVALIER AFGHAN (LE)

170 Prince Arthur East,
Plateau
(514) 284-6662
Authentic Afghan cuisine. Menu
composed of the best traditional
dishes. Specialty: lamb.

KHYBER PASS

506 Duluth East, Plateau
(514) 844-7131
Authentic Afghan cuisine. Try
their mantoo, their samboza as
an entrée, their chopan kebab
(lamb) and the other various
specialities of the house. Typical
decor with several Afghan
photographs and tapestries. Very
friendly owner. Bring your own
wine.

◎ *African*

ABIATA

3435 St. Denis, Plateau
(514) 281-0111
Ethiopian cuisine with a good
selection of vegetarian dishes,
chicken, lamb and beef. Dishes
are served without utensils with
injera bread. The spiciness of the
dishes varies between very spicy
and mild. Exotic African decor.
Don't miss their Ethiopian wine.

AFRICA

837 Mount Royal East,
Plateau
(514) 521-7035
African cuisine with a particular
emphasis on Senegalese

specialties. Cordial environment.
Table d'hôte every day.

MESSOB D'OR (AU)

5690 Monkland, West End
(514) 488-8620
Small Ethiopian restaurant with
40 seats. Specialties: spicy
chicken, steak tartare and lamb.
Try their injera (Ethiopian pita)
and the traditional Ethiopian
coffee.

NIL BLEU (LE)

3706 St. Denis, Plateau
(514) 285-4628
Ethiopian cuisine with a varied
menu. Specialties: lamb, chicken,
seafood and vegetarian dishes.
Exotic decorations and an
intimate environment with a
capacity of 130 people. Open for
more than 10 years.

◎ *Algerian*

COIN BERBÈRE (AU)

73 Duluth East, Plateau
(514) 844-7405
Specialty: couscous. Twenty-two
years of excellence. Cordial and
family environment.

GAZELLE (LA)

201-A, Rachel East, Plateau
(514) 843-9598
One of the best couscouses in
town. Typical Algerian decor.
Possibility of belly dancers upon
request.

RITES BERBÈRES
4697 de Bullion, Plateau
(514) 844-7863
Specialties include an assortment
of aperitifs, méchoui (Quebec
lamb) and house made couscous
served with three kinds of meats.
Two rooms. In business for over
18 years. Bring your own wine.

TAROT (AU)
500 Marie Anne East, Plateau
(514) 849-6860
Authentic Algerian cuisine
specializing in couscous and
lamb. Friendly service. Capacity
of 50.

@ *American*

ISLAND OF MONTREAL

BÂTON ROUGE
180 St. Catherine St. West,
Downtown
(514) 282-7444
Renowned by its customers as a
restaurant with one of the best
rib offerings in town. Very
pleasant service with a taste of
Louisiana. A definite must try.

BÂTON ROUGE
1050 Mountain (de la
Montagne), Downtown
(514) 931-9969

BÂTON ROUGE
3839 St. John's Blvd.,
West Island
(514) 626-6440

BÂTON ROUGE
5385 des Jockeys, West End
(514) 738-1616

BÂTON ROUGE
7999 Blvd. Les Galeries-
d'Anjou, East End
(514) 355-7330
*See also Laval & North Shore
and South Shore*

INDIANA'S
2001 University, Downtown
(514) 845-2002
American restaurant offering
various dishes at an attractive
price. Delicious ribs. Ideal for
family outings or just between
friends.

WINNIE'S
1455 Crescent, Downtown
(514) 288-0623
Varied menu includes pasta,
steaks and hamburgers. Popular
place among business people and
celebrities. Cigars are available.
Open for over 35 years.

LAVAL & NORTH SHORE

BÂTON ROUGE
3035 Blvd. Le Carrefour, Laval
(450) 681-9902
Renowned by its customers as a
restaurant with one of the best
rib offerings in town. Very
pleasant service with a taste of
Louisiana. A definite must try.

SOUTH SHORE

BÂTON ROUGE

4890 Taschereau Blvd.,
Greenfield Park
(450) 466-3100
Renowned by its customers as a
restaurant with one of the best
rib offerings in town. Very
pleasant service with a taste of
Louisiana. A definite must try.

◎ *Anatolian*

LAVAL & NORTH SHORE

CALYPSO

3401 Blvd. Cartier West, Laval
(450) 686-8180
Charming environment.
Specialties: fresh fish, brochettes
and shawarma.

◎ *Asian*

ISLAND OF MONTREAL

ASIE MODERNE

1676 Poirier, North End
(514) 748-0567
Thai, Vietnamese, Kampuchean
and Chinese cuisine. Relaxing
ambiance. Don't miss their
imperial shrimp rolls and the
General Tao chicken.

BAGUETTE D'IVOIRE (LA)

1242 Mackay, Downtown
(514) 932-7099
Vietnamese, Thai and Chinese
restaurant. Specialty: seafood
combo. Excellent basil beef. Good
beer, wine and sake. Asian decor.

FOU D'ASIE

1732 St. Denis, Plateau
(514) 281-0077
Thai, Vietnamese, Kampuchean
and Chinese cuisine. Relaxing
ambiance. Don't miss their
imperial shrimp rolls and the
General Tao chicken.

GINGER

16 Pine Ave. East, Plateau
(514) 844-2121
Asian restaurant with an elegant
decor. Menu presents a variety of
Asian specialties.

SINGAPOUR (LE)

2090 Mountain (de la
Montagne), Downtown
(514) 288-8898
Fine Eastern cuisine. Modern
decor. The noon table d'hôte
includes soup, rolls, rice and
main dish. Specials for two to
four people during the evening.
Open sliding doors during the
summer.

SOY

5258 St. Laurent Blvd.
(St. Lawrence), Plateau
(514) 499-9399
Korean, Thai, Cantonese and
Szechuan cuisine. Table d'hôte
starting at $14. Try the salmon
with sake and Korean BBQ beef.
Unique decor and cordial
ambiance.

TONG POR

43 de la Gauchetière East,
Downtown

(514) 393-9975

Authentic Chinese, Vietnamese
and Thai cuisine. Specialties:
General Tao chicken and duck.
Good selection of noodles.

SOUTH SHORE

ZENDO

450 Blvd. de Mortagne,
Boucherville

(450) 641-8488

Fine Japanese, Vietnamese, Thai,
Szechuan and Pekinese cuisine.
The noon and evening table
d'hôte includes entrée, main dish,
desserts and coffee or tea.
Elegant tatami rooms, shoji
folding screens and sushi counter.

© *Austrian*

VIEUX KITZBUHEL

505 Blvd. Perrot, Ile Perrot

(514) 453-5521

Establishment with a view of the
lake. Austrian, German and
French cuisine. Jovial and cordial
ambiance with Austrian decor.
Traditional Austrian service.

© *Belgian*

ISLAND OF MONTREAL

ACTUEL (L')

1194 Peel, Downtown

(514) 866-1537

Authentic Belgian cuisine. Try the
mussels and shrimp. Very popular
ham & eggs. Family ambiance.

PETIT MOULINSART (LE)

139 St. Paul West,
Old Montreal

(514) 843-7432

Belgian and French bistro of 70
places in business for for over 13
years. Specialty of the house:
mussels. Table d'hôte choices
include: veal chops, fish, tartare
and beef or horse steak. Old
Style decor. 200-year-old house.

WITLOOF (LE)

3619 St. Denis, Plateau

(514) 281-0100

Belgian cuisine. Try the goat's
milk cheese and the salmon (as
an entrée), the chocolate tartare
and the vanilla soup. Don't miss
the mussels and fries. Original
menu. Serene and calm
ambiance.

SOUTH SHORE

**BISTRO DES BIÈRES BELGES
(LE)**

2088 Montcalm, St. Hubert

(450) 465-0669

Specialties: mussels and fries. A
hundred kinds of imported beers.
Centennial building.

© *Bistro*

ISLAND OF MONTREAL

917 (AU)

917 Rachel East, Plateau

(514) 524-0094

Bistro with a typical Parisian
ambiance. Try: lamb, duck breast,

veal sweetbreads and the cheesecake. Enormous portions.

BEAUX JEUDIS (LES)
1449 Crescent, Downtown
(514) 281-5320
Parisian brasserie with a traditional style. Affordable price. Reserve for anniversaries and special events.

BISTRO DÉTOUR
2480 Beaubien East,
North End
(514) 728-3107
French restaurant with a varied menu offering different meats, game and fish. Cordial and elegant place. Picture window. Capacity of 40. Table d'hôte during lunch and dinner.

BISTRO GOURMET (AU)
2100 St. Mathieu, Downtown
(514) 846-1553
Bistro specializing in rack of lamb, rice and veal kidneys (rognons). Capacity of 35. Intimate ambiance. Open for over 12 years.

BISTRO OLIVIERI
5219 Côte des Neiges,
Mount Royal
(514) 739-3303
Bistro serving various styles of cuisine from around the world. Relaxed environment. Ideal for meetings and for family outings.

BISTRO PAPARRAZZI
6846 St. Laurent Blvd.
(St. Lawrence), Downtown
(514) 948-5552
Pasta, salads and sandwiches. Bistro ambiance during the week and rather animated ambiance during weekends. A DJ on Fridays. Daily specials. Capacity of 66.

BISTRO UNIQUE
1039 Beaubien East,
North End
(514) 279-4433
Home-style cuisine with a casual environment and fast service. Everything is homemade: pasta, desserts, bread, etc. Table d'hôte during lunch and dinner includes entrée, main dish and deserts. Specialties: pizzas, pasta and salads. Reception room is available. Open over 20 years.

BORIS BISTRO
465 McGill, Old Montreal
(514) 848-9575
Bistro which has won several Montreal 'Design Commerce' contests for its decor. Specialty: crystallized duck. Large terrasse.

CAFÉ CHERRIER
3635 St. Denis, Plateau
(514) 843-4308
Bistro with a very quaint decor. Ideal for breakfasts.

CAFÉ DES BEAUX-ARTS

1384 Sherbrooke St. West,
Downtown
(514) 843-3233
Fine French cuisine with a pinch of Italian and Portuguese influence. Try the lamb shank, the Portobello mushrooms, the risotto and the roasted scallops. Seats 75. Located on the second floor of the Montreal Museum of Fine Arts main pavillon. Thematic ambiance.

CAFÉ MÉLIÈS

3540 St. Laurent Blvd.
(St. Lawrence), Plateau
(514) 847-9218
Bistro located inside the Ex-Centris complex, with the repertory cinema. Specialties: grilled sirloin steak, bouillabaisse and fish. Lounge serves cocktails, wines and digestives during the evening. Unique decor.

CAFÉ PETIT FLORE

1145 Fleury East, North End
(514) 387-2640
Two sections: restaurant and bar. French cuisine and varied menu. Relaxing ambiance, perfect for outings with friends.

CHEZ PLUME

360 St. Antoine West,
Old Montreal
(514) 987-9900
Bistro with a juke-box. Specialties: light suppers, happy hour (5 to 8 pm) and hamburgers. Small express menu served during lunch. Located in the Intercontinental hotel.

COLBERT (LE)

1235 Jean Talon East,
North End
(514) 271-3890
Fine cuisine. Rustic ambiance. Great selection of pasta, pizzas, veal, grilled meats and seafood. Private rooms for 2 to 50 clients. Perfect for the private parties. Closed Sundays and Mondays.

CONTINENTAL

4169 St. Denis, Plateau
(514) 845-6842
Menu includes pasta, terrine, steaks and blanquette of veal. Continental cuisine influenced by Italian, French and Greek cooking. Bistro-style decor with an artistic touch.

ENTRECÔTE ST-JEAN (L')

2022 Peel, Downtown
(514) 281-6492
Typical Parisian brasserie. Only one dish available: steak frites with soup, salad and dessert. Table d'hôte offered for lunch and dinner. Open every day for over 12 years.

GRAIN DE SEL (LE)

2375 St. Catherine St. East,
East End
(514) 522-5105
Cordial environment and attentive service. French-style bistro-restaurant. Specialty: Maitre Queux's grilled sirloin steak. Variable menu.

GRAND COMPTOIR (LE)

1225 Phillips Square,
Downtown
(514) 393-3295
Charming Parisian bistro. Menu
specials every day for lunch and
dinner include a soup and the
main dish for as little as $10.

GRILL BISTRO 1 (LE)

183 St. Paul East, Old
Montreal
(514) 397-1044
Fine French cuisine. The quality
of service creates the ambiance.
Table d'hôte every day with
specials for lunch. Beautiful
terrasse.

HOLDER

407 McGill Street,
Old Montreal
(514) 849-0333
A bistro par excellence. The
dining room's high ceiling gives
the restaurant a wholesome, airy
feeling. The copper decor
completes the atmosphere. Great
bistro fare.

JAMES ROOSTER ESQ.

3 de la Commune,
Old Montreal
(514) 842-3822
Pub and sports bar. Ambiance is
18th and 19th century, which,
given its history as John McGill's
trading house, makes sense.
Menu items include chicken and
ribs, appetizers and upmarket
sandwiches. Terrasse in the
summer.

MARLOWE

981 St. John's Blvd.,
West Island
(514) 426-8713
St. Lawrence Blvd.-style
restaurant-bar, specializing in
Cajun, Italian and Thai cuisine.

MESS HALL

4858 Sherbrooke St. West,
West End
(514) 482-2167
Recently renovated. Hip
atmosphere with updated fusion
menu. Great burgers and salads.
Quaint terrasse.

MODAVIE

1 St. Paul West, Old Montreal
(514) 287-9582
Jazz shows every day. Specialty:
lamb. More than 300 different
kinds of wine.

MONTCLAIR

747 Decarie Blvd., North End
(514) 747-3227
Original decor: velvet benches
and cement walls. Diversified
music and menu.

MONTRÉALAIS (LE)

900 Blvd. René Lévesque (fka
Dorchester) West, Downtown
(514) 954-2261
Bistro located in the Queen
Elizabeth Hotel. Restaurant and
bar on two levels. Lunch buffet
includes access to the dessert
counter. Beautiful view of the
cathedral.

OPINEL

408 Gilford, Plateau
(514) 848-9696
High class bistro with a capacity
of 50. Pianist on Thursdays and
Fridays. Grilled meats. Wine card
and varied menu.

PARIS-BEURRE (LE)

1226 Van Horne, Mount Royal
(514) 271-7502
Casual Parisian bistro. Specialties:
veal sweetbreads, sirloin steak
and crème brûlée. Lunch and
dinner table d'hôte. Splendid
terrasse with garden.

PETIT EXTRA (AU)

1690 Ontario East, East End
(514) 527-5552
Refined bistro with an excellent
atmosphere that has received
much praise and many favourable
reviews. Varied cuisine: lamb,
chicken, fish, and several choices
of desserts.

P'TIT PLATEAU (LE)

330 Marie Anne East, Plateau
(514) 282-6342
Specialty: dishes from the south-
western part of France.
Traditional ambiance. Closed in
July.

RESTAURANT BISTRO L'ADRESSE

6060 Sherbrooke St. East,
East End
(514) 252-9014
Bistro specializing in trout, veal
and lamb's liver. Capacity of 70.

Wine, beer and spirits. Lunch and
dinner table d'hôte. Modern
decor. French ambiance.

ROSALIE

1232 Mountain (de la
Montagne), Downtown
(514) 392-1970   *$15 to $30*
Trendy French bistro. A touch of
St. Laurent on Mountain St. A
variety of main dishes, including
duck, tuna and rabbit. Large
terrasse in front.

SANS MENU

3714 Notre Dame West,
South End
(514) 933-4782
Beautiful small restaurant with a
menu centered on a fresh
seasonal cuisine. Fast, simple and
cordial service. Perfect for long
evenings between friends.

STEAK FRITES ST-PAUL

12 St. Paul West,
Old Montreal
(514) 842-0972
French cuisine, including
specialties like steak, filet mignon
and a large variety of tapas. Ideal
for business luncheons and
evening outings. Private wine
selection.

See also South Shore.

USINE DE SPAGHETTI PARISIENNE

273 St. Paul East,
Old Montreal
(514) 866-0963
Located in an old building. Menu
à la carte includes several
specials. Good variety of pasta.

YOYO

4720 Marquette, Plateau
(514) 524-4187
Fine French cuisine. Specialties:
veal and lamb sweetbread. Bring
your own wine. Capacity of 70.
Cordial ambiance.

LAVAL & NORTH SHORE

BISTRO LE MOUTON NOIR

30 Blvd. Curé Labelle, Laval
(450) 628-8176
Centennial house converted into
a two floor restaurant. Warm and
casual ambiance with a rustic
decor. Two fireplaces. Varied
table d'hôte and menu. Specialty:
pasta.

PRIMA NOTTE

500 Blvd. St. Martin West,
Laval
(450) 975-7555
Italian bistro specializing in
homemade pasta. Calm and
romantic ambiance during dinner
and perfect for business
luncheons.

SOUTH SHORE

BISTRO LE VIEUX BOURGOGNE

1718 Bourgogne, Chambly
(450) 447-9306
Open only for lunch. Antique
decor.

CAFÉ TERRASSE 1957

305 St. Charles West,
Longueuil
(450) 928-4628
Great selection of Unibroue beer.
Casual ambiance. Specialties:
croc 57 and hamburgers.

MAGIA (LA)

361 St. Charles West,
Longueuil
(450) 670-7131
Typically Italian bistro specializing
in pasta and pizzas. Lively
ambiance. Table d'hôte
during lunch.

STEAK FRITES ST-PAUL

95 Blvd. de Mortagne,
Boucherville
(450) 655-1808
French cuisine. Steak, filet
mignon. Also, a large variety of
tapas. Ideal for business
luncheons and evening outings.
Private wine selection.

TIRE-BOUCHON (LE)
141 Blvd. de Mortagne,
Boucherville
(450) 449-6112
Parisian-style bistro. Mix of
French, Mediterranean and North
African cuisine.

◎ *Café*

CAFÉ DES ECLUSIERS
Parc des Ecluses,
Old Montreal
(514) 496-9767
Open café located in Old
Montreal. Considered by locals to
be one of the best '5 à 7' happy
hour hotspots of the city.
Terrasse available.

CAFÉ DU NOUVEAU MONDE
84 St. Catherine St. West,
Downtown
(514) 866-8669
French restaurant located inside
of the Théâtre du Nouveau
Monde. Two floors. Nominee of
the Montreal 'Design Commerce'
contest.

CAFÉ ET BOUFFE
171 Villeray, North End
(514) 277-7455
Local bistro. Hidden on a quiet
street of the Villeray district.
Menu includes sandwiches,
salads and pasta. Casual
ambiance.

CAFÉ FLEURI
1255 Jeanne Mance,
Downtown
(514) 285-1450
Restaurant located inside of the
Wyndham Hotel, in the
Desjardins Complex. View of the
hotel gardens. Breakfast, lunch &
buffet.

COTÉ SOLEIL
3979 St. Denis, Plateau
(514) 282-8037
Specialties: grilled sirloin steak,
mussels and rack of lamb. Cordial
ambiance. Two terrasses during
the summer. Diversified wine list.

◎ *Cajun/Creole/Caribbean*

BENEDICTS
5950 Monkland, West End
(514) 481-6075
Local restaurant with a casual
ambiance. Breakfast served seven
days a week. Menu includes
swordfish, salmon, chicken and a
large salad served with papayas
and mangos. Try their table
d'hôte. Complete bar.

LOUISIANE (LA)
5850 Sherbrooke St. West,
West End
(514) 369-3073
Open-style kitchen and bar.
Intimate ambiance. Candlelight
dinners. New Orleans-style menu:
crab, Cajun chicken, jambalaya
and blackened fish. Jazz and
blues.

PARADIS DES AMIS (LE)

1751 Fullum, East End
(514) 525-6861
West Indian gastronomy.
Caribbean decor (palm trees).
Specialties: lobster, fresh
seafood, fish and game. Alcohol
license and wine list.
Reservations are possible for
special events.

◎ *Chinese*

ISLAND OF MONTREAL

BEIJING

92 de la Gauchetière East,
East End
(514) 861-2003
Cantonese and Szechuan cuisine.
Specialties: noodles and seafood.
More than 10 different varieties
of fish and homemade noodles.

BILL WONG

7965 Decarie Blvd,
Mount Royal
(514) 731-8202
Szechuan and Cantonese buffet at
an affordable price. Modern
ambiance. Delivery service
available.

BON BLÉ RIZ

1437 St. Laurent Blvd. (St.
Lawrence), Downtown
(514) 844-1447
Fine Szechuan cuisine.
Homemade noodles. Menu offers
a great selection of seafood. Try
the candy chicken (crispy with a
honey spiced sauce). Open for

over 20 years. Reservation
required for groups.

CAVEAU SZECHWAN (LE)

6000 Monkland, West End
(514) 488-2818
Szechuan specialties: General Tao
chicken, sesame beef or orange
beef, Szechuan shrimp. Chinese
beer (tsingtao) and sake. Modern
decor. Delivery available in NDG
and the immediate area.

CHINE TOQUE

4050 St. Catherine St. West,
West End
(514) 989-5999
Chinese and Szechuan cuisine.
Try their peppered chicken with
spinach and their Szechuan
shrimp. Table d'hôte during lunch.
Menu à la carte with combos for
two people during evenings.
Contemporary decor.

CHOW'S

335 Dorval, West Island
(514) 636-4770
Szechuan and Chinese buffet.
Open from 11 am to 2 pm and
from 5 pm to 9 pm. Polynesian
decor. Capacity of 90 clients.
Local and Chinese (tsingtao)
beers, sake and cocktails.

CHRYSANTHÈME

1208 Crescent, Downtown
(514) 397-1408
Fine Szechuan cuisine. Try the
won-ton raviolis in a spicy ginger
sauce and the spicy lamb.
Beautiful decor.

COPINES DE CHINE

870 de Maisonneuve East,
East End
(514) 842-8325
Fine Szechuan and Japanese
cuisine. Specialties: Hunan
dumplings, sushi, sashimi and
General Tao Chicken. Chinese
(tsingtao) and Japanese (sapporo)
beers. Delivery and take-out
service available.

DÉLICES DE SZECHUAN (AUX)

1735 St. Denis, Downtown
(514) 844-5542
Szechuan, Vietnamese and Thai
cuisine. Menu includes General
Tao chicken, small rolls and
Hunan dumplings. Good selection
of alcohol: sake, beers and wines.
Open for over 20 years.

ENVOL DE CHINE (L')

398 boul. René Lévesque (fka
Dorchester) West, Downtown
(514) 866-8788
Szechuan and Thai cuisine.
General Tao chicken, Hunan
dumplings and Thai shrimp.
Imported alcohol: tsingtao
and sake.

FINESSES D'ORIENT

1000 St. John's Blvd.,
West Island
(514) 630-0101
Szechuan and Thai cuisine. All
you can eat buffet or menu à la
carte. Modern decor. Try the
General Tao chicken and the Thai
shrimp.

FINESSES D'ORIENT

38 Pl. du Commerce,
Nun's Island
(514) 768-1888

FU KAM WAH

1180 Decarie, West End
(514) 337-2262
Authentic Chinese cuisine. Fresh
fish in black bean sauce, Dim
Sum, whole wok-fried crab, crispy
duck and much more. Reasonable
prices, great food in a casual
setting.

GOURMET HOT & SPICY (LE)

7373 Decarie Blvd., Mount
Royal
(514) 731-1818
Varied choices at the buffet.
Modern decor with an Asian
touch. Try: shrimp on bread,
General Tao chicken and the
sesame beef. Menu à la carte is
available during lunch and the
dinner buffet is $23.

JARDIN DU NORD

78 de la Gauchetière West,
Downtown
(514) 395-8023
Fine Pekinese and Szechuan
cuisine. Menu offers an
enormous choice including
Pekinese duck, Pekinese ribs and
pok choy (vegetable dish). Wine,
beer and spirits and large variety
of alcohol: wines, tsingtao, sake,
sapporo and local beers.

KAM FUNG (LA MAISON)
1936 Blvd. Thimens,
North End
(514) 856-9288
Szechuan and Cantonese cuisine.
Excellent quality/price value.
Menu composed of several
popular dishes and seafood.
Asian ambiance and Chinese
music. Reservations are possible
for anniversaries.

KAMLUNT
2500 Blvd. Henri Bourassa
East, North End
(514) 389-8263
Buffet and menu à la carte
specializing in Szechuan and
Cantonese cuisine. Traditional
Chinese decor. Family ambiance.
Open every day. Delivery
available. 10 % reduction on
take-out orders.

LOTTÉ
1115 Clark, Downtown
(514) 393-3838
Szechuan and Cantonese cuisine.
Excellent crab. Also, Chinese
combos (set of Szechuan,
Cantonese and Thai dishes).
Wine, beer and spirits.
Contemporary ambiance.

LUCK HOP FOO
5214 St. Laurent Blvd.
(St. Lawrence), Plateau
(514) 948-5503
Fine Szechuan and Cantonese
cuisine. Specialties: Hunan
dumplings, General Tao chicken,
orange beef and soups. Modern

decor with an Asian touch.
Delivery service available.

MAISON GUANG ZHOU (LA)
84 de la Gauchetière West,
Downtown
(514) 397-9410
Cantonese and Szechuan cuisine.
Specialties: lobster, crab, oysters
and mussels. Try their lamb
fondue. Casual Asian-style
ambiance.

MAISON VIP (LA)
1077 Clark, Downtown
(514) 861-1943
Small restaurant offering
Szechuan and Cantonese style
cuisine. Varied menu. Specialties:
seafood and traditional dishes.
Excellent beef soup. Simple and
family oriented ambiance.
Excellent for an outing between
friends.

MER JAUNE (LA)
5832 Blvd. Léger, North End
(514) 324-6511
Szechuan and Chinese cuisine.
Specialty: butterfly shrimp. Try
their special of the day. Antique
decor with a Chinese touch.
Delivery service available.

MR. MA
1 Pl. Ville Marie, Downtown
(514) 866-8000
Szechuan and Cantonese
restaurant. Specialties: dim sum
and seafood. Capacity of 220. A
very casual yet elegant ambiance,
perfect for romantic or business
dinners. Traditional decor.

Experienced service. Free parking after 5:30 pm.

NEW DYNASTY

1110 Clark, Downtown
(514) 871-8778
Cantonese and Szechuan restaurant. Nice Asian decor. Very varied menu. Specialties: lobster and oysters. Take-out service available.

NOUVEAU PARADIS (LE)

13035 Sherbrooke St. East,
East End
(514) 642-0433
Menu includes Cambodian, Chinese and Thai dishes. Elegant Asian ambiance. Specials during lunch and the dinner table d'hôte includes a soup, rolls, main dish, dessert and coffee.

ON LUCK

1701 Sources Blvd.,
West Island
(514) 636-0660
Fast but tasty Chinese cuisine. Menu includes all the popular dishes. Good quality/price value. Take-out service available.

ORICHINE

1798 Blvd. St. Joseph,
West Island
(514) 639-1800
Szechuan cuisine: General Tao chicken, shrimp, pad Thai and orange beef. Variety of local and Chinese beers, wine and sake. Modern decor with an Asian touch. Take-out service available.

PALAIS IMPÉRIAL (LE)

120 du Barry, West Island
(514) 426-3888
Buffet and menu à la carte. Szechuan, Cantonese and Thai specialties. Menu includes a large variety of dishes. Capacity of 80 clients. Modern decor with a Chinese touch. Delivery service available.

PAPILLON BLEU

200 St. Jacques West,
Old Montreal
(514) 849-8499
Szechuan and Cantonese restaurant with a casual ambiance. Located near the Notre Dame Basilica. Possibility of reservations for parties. Closed on Sundays. Delivery service available.

PAPILLON DE SZECHUAN

5404 Queen Mary,
Mount Royal
(514) 487-1459
Buffet and menu à la carte with table d'hôte available. Excellent Chinese-style filet mignon. Two sections of 80 seats. Friendly ambiance in a modern decor.

PARASOL CHINOIS (AU)

325 Blvd. Henri Bourassa
East, North End
(514) 384-1070
Szechuan and Cantonese cuisine. Menu à la carte only. Specialty includes General Tao chicken and orange chicken. Modern decor. Family ambiance. Open every day

for lunch and dinner. Open for over 25 years.

PAVILLON NANPIC (LE)

75-A, de la Gauchetière West, Downtown
(514) 395-8106
Menu with an abundant choice of dishes. Excellent Hunan dumplings and delicious orange beef. Modern ambiance with an Asian influence. Delivery service available on weekends only.

PERLE (LA)

4230 St. John's Blvd., West Island
(514) 624-6010
Szechuan and Thai cuisine. Buffet served at your table and menu à la carte. Renowned for its General Tao chicken and its Hunnan dumplings.
Contemporary decor and casual ambiance.

RESTAURANT SZECHUAN

400 Notre Dame West, Old Montreal
(514) 844-4456
Cordial bistro with a modest decor. Friendly service. Specialties include honey chicken, double cooked pork, lamb with Hunan sauce and other treats. Generous portions.

SHANGHAI (LE)

2028 St. Denis, Plateau
(514) 982-6711
Fine Szechuan cuisine. Excellent menu à la carte. Specialties:

Shanghai duck and black peppered shrimp with ginger and green onions. Typical Chinese ambiance. Capacity of 100 clients.

SZECHUAN PALACE

3964 St. Denis, Plateau
(514) 499-1668
Elegant fine Chinese and Thai cuisine restaurant. Menu à la carte and an all you can eat sampling menu is also available. Specialties: Hunan dumplings and the roasted banana chicken. Casual ambiance. Good wine menu.

TAO

374 Victoria, West End
(514) 369-1122
Menu composed of all the Cantonese, Szechuan and Thai popular contemporary specialties. Simple decor.

TCHANG KIANG

6066 Sherbrooke St. West, West End
(514) 487-7744
Szechuan and Cantonese restaurant. Specialties: Hunan dumplings, orange beef and peppered chicken. Modern decor and family ambiance. Open for over 28 years.

VAN ROY

1095 Clark, Downtown
(514) 871-1724
Fine cuisine. Specialty: seafood. Try their lobster, oysters and mussels. Elegant decor and plush

ambiance. Open for over 30 years.

VILLAGE MON NAN

1098 Clark, Downtown
(514) 879-9680
Shanghai and Peking region cuisine. Specialties: Peking duck and Shanghai style dim sum. Diversified menu. Typical Asian decor. Capacity of 100.

WAH-DO

4054 St. Catherine St. East, East End (514) 524-3917
Cantonese and Szechuan menu à la carte and buffet. Specialty: Cantonese chow mein. Wine, beer and spirits. Delivery service is available. Open for over 30 years.

WING FA

3474 Park Ave., Plateau
(514) 282-3938
Authentic fine Chinese cuisine restaurant. Diversified and affordably priced menu. Wine, beer and spirits. Cordial ambiance and a typical Asian decor. Capacity of 60. Open for over 15 years.

WOK DE SZECHUAN (LE)

1950 Fleury East, North End
(514) 382-2060
Fine Szechuan cuisine. Menu offers a vast range of dishes. Specialties: Hunan dumplings, General Tao chicken and orange beef. Wine, beer and spirits. Capacity of 100 clients. Cordial ambiance and comfortable.

Closed on Mondays. Open for over 20 years.

ZEN

1050 Sherbrooke St. West, Downtown
(514) 499-0801
Fine Szechuan cuisine. Two menus: days and evenings. Table d'hôte during the day is between $15 and $22. Menu à la carte at a fixed price ($29). Choice of 40 various dishes. Very contemporary decor. Two private rooms able to accommodate 60 clients in all.

LAVAL & NORTH SHORE

DÉLICES DE CHINE (LES)

4225 Samson, Laval
(450) 688-2450
Szechuan and Cantonese cuisine. Excellent Cantonese chow mein, butterfly shrimp and General Tao chicken. Roomy and cordial ambiance. Modern decor. Delivery and take-out service available.

FINESSES D'ORIENT

2560-A Blvd. Daniel Johnson, Laval
(450) 686-0902
Szechuan and Cantonese cuisine. Sampling menu (buffet-style but brought to your table) and menu à la carte are available. Try: peanut butter dumplings. Capacity from 150 to 200 clients.

SAM SING
7782 Blvd. Lévesque East,
Laval
(450) 664-2777
Chinese and Canadian restaurant
with a good variety of dishes:
chop suey, General Tao chicken,
orange beef and soups. Family
ambiance with an Asian decor.
Capacity of 50. Delivery service
available.

© *Creperie*

CRÊPERIE CHEZ SUZETTE
3 St. Paul East, Old Montreal
(514) 874-1984
Restaurant on three floors
specializing in crêpes, gratins,
Swiss fondue and other dishes.
Crêpe-meal and crêpe-desserts
with toppings of your choice.
Wine list and complete bar.
Cordial ambiance in a pastoral-
style decor. Capacity of 150.

JARDIN NELSON (LE)
407 Pl. Jacques Cartier,
Old Montreal
(514) 861-5731
Pancake restaurant located in the
heart of the Old Montreal. Menu
composed of crêpes, pizzas,
salads, etc. Casual ambiance and
musicians depending on the
weather (classical music or jazz).
Large terrasse. Open for over 25
years.

© *Deli*

Island of Montreal

MOE'S DELI & BAR
3950 Sherbrooke St. East,
East End
(514) 253-6637
Large restaurant. Specialties: ribs,
smoked meat and steaks. Full
service bar. Happy hour from 4
pm to 8 pm from Monday to
Friday. Located in the heart of
Montreal. Good wine list.
Excellent ambiance for business
luncheons.

MOE'S DELI & BAR
6795 Jarry East, East End
(514) 322-6637

MOE'S DELI & BAR
940 St. John's Blvd.,
West Island
(514) 426-8247
See also Laval & North Shore

SNOWDON DELI
5265 Decarie Blvd., Mount
Royal
(514) 488-9129
Delicatessen. Specialties: smoked
meat and homemade soups.
Complete breakfasts served
everyday. Capacity of 100 clients.
Fast and courteous service.
Delivery available.

MOE'S DELI & BAR
380 Blvd. St. Martin West,
Laval
(450) 975-4960
Large restaurant. Specialties: ribs,
smoked meat and steaks. Full
service bar. Happy hour from 4
pm to 8 pm from Monday to
Friday. Located in the heart of
Montreal. Good wine list.
Excellent ambiance for business
luncheons.

© *Fast Food*

ISLAND OF MONTREAL

ANECDOTE (L')
801 Rachel East, Plateau
(514) 526-7967
Snack bar serving old-style
hamburgers. Popular place.
Somewhat of a retro decor.

CARTET (LE)
106 McGill, Old Montreal
(514) 871-8887
Bistro with simple yet chic
ambiance (grocery-style). The
menu is presented on a
blackboard. Dishes are prepared
with great care.

FRISCO BAR & GRILL
405 St. Antoine West,
Old Montreal
(514) 866-0935
Restaurant located between Old
Montreal and the downtown area.
Specialties: pasta, roast beef and
couscous. Modern decor.

GOELETTE (LA)
8551 St. Laurent Blvd.
(St. Lawrence), North End
(514) 388-8393
Canadian cuisine specializing in
seafood and steaks. Alcohol
license and a good wine menu.
Reception room and parking
available.

JAVA U
4914 Sherbrooke St. West,
West End
(514) 482-7077
Menu composed of Viennese
pastries, brioches and other
types of pastries. Casual
ambiance with a sophisticated
decor. Not unlike a bistro.

L'APARTÉ
5029 St. Denis, Plateau
(514) 282-0911
A wide variety of coffee brands.
Fast service at an affordable
price: couscous, sandwiches and
grilled meats. Small terrasse.

MA-AM-M BOLDUC
4351 de Lorimier, Plateau
(514) 527-3884
Small typical Quebec-style
restaurant. Breakfast. Special of
the day includes soup, main dish,
dessert and coffee.

PARYSE (LA)
302 Ontario East, Downtown
(514) 842-2040
Small bistro that mainly serves
hamburgers. High quality and fast
service. Open for over 20 years.

RIVOLI

7275 Sherbrooke St. East,
East End
(514) 353-0440
Specialties: pasta, filet mignon
and surf 'n' turf. Romantic and
intimate ambiance.

SOUTH SHORE

LAURENCE

578 St. Charles, Boucherville
(450) 641-1564
Small French and Quebec style
cuisine. Menu focused on fine
country-style cooking. Rustic
ambiance with a fireplace. Table
d'hôte starting from $10 during
lunch and $20 during dinner.

ⓖ *Fondue*

ISLAND OF MONTREAL

FONDERIE (LA)

964 Rachel East, Plateau
(514) 524-2100
Specialties: Chinese and
bourguignon fondues. 110 places
divided into two rooms. Open at
5 pm everyday. Centennial house
with a period decor. Restaurant in
business for over 22 years.

FONDERIE LAJEUNESSE (LA)

10145 Lajeunesse, North End
(514) 382-8234
Restaurant specializing in
fondues: chocolate, cheese,
bourguignon and Chinese. Two
floors able to accommodate 350
clients. Closed on Mondays.

Various tables d'hôte offered for
dinner.

FONDUE DU PRINCE (LA)

94 St. Anne, West Island
(514) 457-6278
Menu mostly composed of
fondues, but also offers steaks,
grilled meats and fish. Beautiful
view of the water bank. Romantic
ambiance with a fireplace. Open
evenings only. Excellent wine list
(private selection).

FONDUE MENTALE

4325 St. Denis, Plateau
(514) 499-1446
Specialty of the house: fondue of
game meats (stag, caribou and
wild boar). Also, several other
types of fondues. Authentic
Victorian decor. Two dining
rooms wit a country cottage
style. The garden is open during
the summer.

FONDUES DU ROI (LES)

6754 Jarry East, East End
(514) 955-9928
Establishment with karaoke
evenings and dinner-dancing.
Menu composed of chocolate,
bourguignon and cheese fondues.
Capacity of 180 clients. Disco-bar
style decor.

LAVAL & NORTH SHORE

JARDIN DES FONDUES

186 St. Marie, Terrebonne
(450) 492-2048
Fine restaurant specializing in
fondues. Capacity of 65. Table

d'hôte offered every evening. Romantic ambiance with a terrasse during the summer.

© *French*

ISLAND OF MONTREAL

5e PÉCHÉ (LE)
330 Mount Royal East, Plateau
(514) 286-0123
Local bistro with a French touch. Only fresh products are used. Casual ambiance. Excellent wine list.

ACADÉMIE (L')
4051 St. Denis, Plateau
(514) 849-2249
French and Italian cuisine. Cordial ambiance. Lunch and dinner table d'hôte that includes soup, salad, main dish and coffee. Affordable prices. Bring your own wine.

ANISE
104 Laurier West, Plateau
(514) 276-6999
French cuisine. Try their entrée of roasted octopus or their surf 'n' turf with anise. Main dishes include duck breast, quail, ratatouille and saddle of lamb. Wide selection of cheeses. Comprehensive wine list. Seating for 60.

APRÈS LE JOUR
901 Rachel East, Plateau
(514) 527-4141
French cuisine. Plush ambiance, bar lounge-style with jazz music.

Try their rice and their veal kidneys. Homemade desserts. Reception room. Capacity of 120 clients. Bring your own wine.

ARRIVAGE (L')
350 Pl. Royale, Old Montreal
(514) 872-9128
Restaurant of fine French cuisine. Try the cranberry duck. Courteous and attentive service. Beautiful ambiance and the windows offer a beautiful view of the port.

BERGAMOTE (LA)
2101 Sherbrooke St. East, East End
(514) 525-5738
Fine market-style cuisine. Good selection of fresh fish and game meats. Charming and romantic decor with stone walls. Capacity of 40 clients. Wine, beer and spirits.

BISTINGO (LE)
1199 Van Horne, Mount Royal
(514) 270-6162
Varied French menu. Try their calf brains, their grilled sirloin steak and their tournedos of salmon. French decor with an intimate ambiance. Good wine list.

BISTRO DU ROY (LE)
3784 de Mentana, Plateau
(514) 525-1624
Fine French restaurant specializing in meat offals, game meats, filet mignon and other traditional dishes. Beautiful environment, ideal for a brunch

between friends. Bring your own wine.

BISTRO GOURMET 2 (AU)

4007 St. Denis, Plateau
(514) 844-0555
French specialties with a diversified menu. Dishes presented with style. Try the roasted sirloin steak and the lamb. Traditional decor with a bistro ambiance. Terrasse of 25 places open in the summer. Pleasant service.

BISTRO L'ENTREPONT

4622 Hôtel de Ville, Plateau
(514) 845-1369
Fine French cuisine. Two services, at 6 pm or at 9 pm. Fridays and Saturdays. Open on Sundays only during the winter season. Entirely nonsmoking.

BOHÈME (LA)

3625 St. Denis, Plateau
(514) 286-6659
Diversified main dishes: grilled sirloin steak, couscous, shank and salmon. Wood decorations give this restaurant a pleasant ambiance. Capacity of 50 clients. Open for over 16 years.

BOUQUET (LE)

450 Sherbrooke St. West, Downtown
(514) 286-1986
Specialties: poultry, rack of lamb, seafood. Table d'hôte during evenings. Capacity of 100. Serene ambiance with jazz music. Breakfast served every day.

BÉCANE ROUGE (LA)

4316 St. Catherine St. East, East End
(514) 252-5420
Fine cuisine with a varied menu: confit of duck, blood sausage, game meats. Intimate and inviting ambiance. Casual environment. Good wine menu (Private selection of imported wine).

CHAMBERTIN (LE)

9 Frontenac, West Island
(514) 695-0620
Menu composed of various dishes: steaks, seafood, etc. Beautiful ambiance with a duet of musicians from Friday to Sunday. Ideal for business dinners during lunch. Capacity of 170 clients.

CHANDELIER (LE)

825 Blvd. Côte-Vertu, North End
(514) 748-5800
French restaurant with a good quality/price value. Romantic ambiance with a fireplace.

CHAZ RESTO-BAR

100 ch. de la Pointe Nord, Nun's Island
(514) 769-9989
Fine restaurant specializing in confit of duck. Beautiful romantic ambiance with a view of the downtown area. Capacity of 200 clients. Possibility of receptions.

CHEZ BEAUCHESNE

3971 Hochelaga, East End
(514) 257-9274
Restaurant with a bistro
ambiance. Capacity of 65 clients.
Table d'hôte for lunch and dinner.
Filtered lighting. Catering service
available.

CHEZ BONNIN

7828 St. Hubert, North End
(514) 272-9031
French restaurant with a rustic
and intimate ambiance.
Courteous service. Specialties of
the house: rack of lamb, the
fisherman plate. Good
quality/price value. Generous
portions.

CHEZ GAUTIER

3487 Park Ave., Plateau
(514) 845-2992
Restaurant-bistro with a Parisian
ambiance. Varied menu: veal
liver, leg of lamb, raw mahi mahi,
tartare, etc. Table d'hôte during
lunch and dinner.

CHEZ LÉVÈQUE

1030 Laurier West,
Mount Royal
(514) 279-7355
Classic French restaurant-
brasserie. Diversified menu: veal
sweetbread, bouillabaisse, blood
sausage. Snow crabs are a must.
Two floors with a capacity of 120
clients. Great French wine
selection (200 to 300). Open for
over 30 years. Reception service
is also offered.

CHEZ PIERRE

1263 Labelle, East End
(514) 843-5227
Traditional restaurant. Menu
composed of offals: veal liver,
kidneys, etc. Intimate ambiance,
ideal for couples and for business
people. Private room available.

COLOMBE (LA)

554 Duluth East, Plateau
(514) 849-8844
French cuisine. Entirely
nonsmoking. Intimate ambiance.
French specialties with a varied
menu. Capacity of 36. Closed on
Mondays. Bring your own wine.

DALI MATISSE

900 Duluth East, Plateau
(514) 845-6557
Bring your own wine. French and
international cuisine. Try their
game meat triad (stag, pheasant,
ostrich), the skate and paella of
Valencia. Seats 50. Terrasse of
20 places open in the summer.
Cordial decor; bistro ambiance.

DES GOUVERNEURS

458 Pl. Jacques Cartier,
Old Montreal
(514) 861-0188
Cuisine with a variety of dishes:
rack of lamb, lobster, frog legs
and veal. Seats 65. Intimate
ambiance with stone walls and a
little wood. Table d'hôte offered
for lunch and dinner. Good wine
selection.

DEUX CHARENTES (LES)

815 de Maisonneuve East,
East End
(514) 523-1132
French cuisine influenced by the
Charente region of France.
Different table d'hôte for lunch
and dinner. Capacity of 60. Brick
walls with a chimney and a real
fireplace. Friendly ambiance,
perfect for couples. Wine list with
268 choices of wines.

DÉCOUVERTE (LA)

4350 de La Roche, Plateau
(514) 529-8377
Fine cuisine specializing in filet of
lamb, calf brains and duck.
Friendly and casual decor.
Capacity of 50. Table d'hôte is
served only at night. Bring your
own wine.

ENTRE-MICHE (L')

2275 St. Catherine St. East,
East End
(514) 521-0036
Classic bistro. Refined cuisine
with friendly service.

FLAMBARD (LE)

851 Rachel East, Plateau
(514) 596-1280
Small local French restaurant
specializing in cassoulet, confit of
duck and rack of lamb. Capacity
of 40 clients. Friendly ambiance.
Open every day. Bring your own
wine.

FLOCON (LE)

540 Duluth East, Plateau
(514) 844-0713
Restaurant that seats 75.
Sophisticated decor but cordial
ambiance. Table d'hôte in the
evenings, with two or four
services. Different menu each
month. Open for over 20 years.
Bring your own wine.

GARGOTE (LA)

351 Pl. d'Youville,
Old Montreal
(514) 844-1428
Restaurant of fine authentic
French cuisine. Good
quality/price value. Cordial
ambiance with a fireplace.

GAVROCHE (LE)

2098 Jean Talon East,
North End
(514) 725-9077
Fine French cuisine with a varied
menu: game meats, meat offals
and a variety of prepared dishes.
Table d'hôte offered during lunch
and dinner. Family ambiance.

GRAND CAFÉ (LE)

1181 Union, Downtown
(514) 866-1303
Fine French cuisine with game
meats and a good selection of
offal. Table d'hôte offered during
lunch and dinner. Cordial
ambiance with an elegant decor.
Possibility of reception for
groups. Good wine selection.

HÉRITIERS (LES)

5091 de Lanaudière, Plateau
(514) 528-4953
Restaurant specializing in meat offals. Menu à la carte only and menus for small groups are available. Casual ambiance. Bring your own wine.

INDÉPENDANT (L')

1330 St. Catherine St. East, East End
(514) 527-3045
Small French restaurant of 50 places specializing in mussels and fondues. Only has a table d'hôte during the evening. Closed for lunch. Family atmosphere, regular customers.

INFIDÈLES (LES)

771 Rachel East, Plateau
(514) 528-8555
French cuisine with a menu made up of several specialties, in particular veal sweetbread and scallops. Generous servings. Courteous and friendly service.

JOLI MOULIN (LE)

5780 Sherbrooke St. East, East End
(514) 254-2125
Restaurant specializing in seafood and grilled meats. The chef's selection: the roast beef. Daily special everyday. Chic ambiance. Capacity of 175.

MAISTRE (LE)

5700 Monkland, West End
(514) 481-2109
Varied cuisine with specialties from the southwestern part of France. Diversified menu. Specials on Tuesdays and Wednesdays including a table d'hôte at $27. Reception room of 50 places. Convivial ambiance with a fireplace. Ideal for couples.

MARGAUX (LE)

371 Villeneuve East, Plateau
(514) 289-9921
Small restaurant specializing in partridge and duck breast. Simple decor with an intimate and friendly ambiance. Wine, beer, and spirits. Closed on Sundays and Mondays.

MICHAEL W.

2601 Centre, South End
(514) 931-0821
Franco-Italian restaurant specializing in game meats. Try their pears, the ceviche and their crème brûlée. Beautiful terrasse. Four dining rooms with a total capacity of 75 clients. Pleasant and intimate ambiance. Bring your own wine.

PARIS (LE)

1812 St. Catherine St. West, Downtown
(514) 937-4898
Establishment open since 1956. Restaurant specializing in pork offal. Casual ambiance with a bistro theme. Capacity of 115.

PEN CASTEL

1224 Ranger, North End
(514) 331-4945
French restaurant specializing in
game meats. Cordial and intimate
ambiance. Small restaurant of 35
places. Table d'hôte served
during lunch and dinner. Flowered
terrasse. Large parking lot.

PETIT RESTO (AU)

4650 de Mentana, Plateau
(514) 598-7963
Specialties: duck-liver pâté, confit
of duck, hazelnut lamb and filet
mignon with blue ermite sauce.
Capacity of 45 clients.
Reservations are preferable. Table
d'hôte changes each week. Open
for over 17 years. Bring your own
wine.

PIED DE COCHON (AU)

536 Duluth East, Plateau
(514) 281-1114
Classic bistro decor of the 1930's.
Interesting menu with a very
original presentation. Traditional
French dishes. Try the stag
tartare, the confit of duck and the
beef stew with fish. Attentive
service. Open-style kitchen.

PITON DE LA FOURNAISE (LE)

835 Duluth East, Plateau
(514) 526-3936
Exotic cuisine specializing in
gastronomy from Reunion Island.
Menu has an Indian and African
influence. Picturesque and
cordial. Open only in the
evenings. Bring your own wine.

PREMIÈRE RUE (LA)

355 St. Paul West,
Old Montreal
(514) 285-0022
Nice small and casual restaurant
of 35 places. French cuisine with
only a table d'hôte.

PRUNELLE (LA)

327 Duluth East, Plateau
(514) 849-8403
Fine French cuisine. Warm and
distinguished environment. Large
sliding doors that open on Duluth
in the summer. Bring your own
wine.

P'TIT LYONNAIS (LE)

1279 Marie Anne East, Plateau
(514) 523-2424
Small restaurant of fine Lyon-
naisse cuisine. Impeccable and
personalized service. Intimate
ambiance. Excellent table d'hôte.

PÉGASE (LE)

1831 Gilford, Plateau
(514) 522-0487
Small restaurant of 34 places.
Gourmet menu includes a soup, a
salad, an entrée, the main dish,
dessert and a coffee. Calm
ambiance during the week and
animated on weekends. Bring
your own wine.

QUARTIER ST LOUIS
4723 St. Denis, Plateau
(514) 284-7723
French cuisine with a taste of the south of France. Cordial and family ambiance. Choice between 14 different tables d'hôtes. Highly commended by critics.

RAPIÈRE (LA)
1155 Metcalfe, Downtown
(514) 871-8920
Establishment located in the Sun Life building. Cordial, inviting ambiance, specializing in Pyrenees cuisine. Business luncheons during midday, closed on Sundays. Open for over 30 years.

RESTAURANT AUBERGE DU CHEVAL BLANC
15760 Notre Dame East, East End (514) 642-4091
French cuisine specializing in game and grilled meats. Capacity of 60. Inn-style ambiance. Intimate and cordial atmosphere. Guitarist on Thursdays, Fridays and Saturdays starting at 6:30 pm: classical music.

RESTO GUY ET DODO MORALI
1444 Metcalfe, Downtown
(514) 842-3636
Fine cuisine specializing in confit of duck. Welcoming ambiance with a private room for 18 people. Table d'hôte offered during lunch and dinner; 114 wines. Internal and external terrasse. Indoor parking. Open for over 25 years.

ROBERT ET COMPAGNIE
2095 McGill College, Downtown
(514) 849-2742
Chic bistro offering a cordial ambiance and decorated like a cathedral. Varied menu, composed of traditional dishes: tilapia, confit of duck and salads.

ROTONDE (LA)
185 St. Catherine St. West, Downtown
(514) 847-6900
Cuisine of Provence. Specialties: 'encornet à la sétoise', duck breast glazed in honey and lavender and shepherd style rack of lamb. Good selection of desserts. Beautiful and large terrasse.

SAUVAGINE (LA)
115 St. Paul East, Old Montreal
(514) 861-3210
French cuisine with a good wine selection. Menu composed of several specialties, including game meats. Courteous service.

SOUBISE (LE)
1184 Crescent, Downtown
(514) 861-8791
Classic ambiance with a lounge, a meridian room with ceramics and a very intimate bar. French and Italian cuisine.

SURCOUF
51 St. Anne de Bellevue,
West Island
(514) 457-6699
Old Canadian house divided into
three different rooms. Charming
and rustic. Solarium during the
summer and a fireplace during
the winter.

TONNERRE DE BREST
1134 Van Horne, Mount Royal
(514) 278-6061
Small restaurant of 24 places,
very family oriented. Fine French
cuisine of Brittany. Fresh
ingredients directly from the
market.

TROIS SOEURS (LES)
479 Beaconsfield, West Island
(514) 694-6731
Fine contemporary French
cuisine. Intimate ambiance: old
house converted into a
restaurant. Table d'hôte changes
each evening. Reception room for
35 people on the second floor.

VAUQUELIN (LE)
52 St. Jacques, Old Montreal
(514) 845-1575
Fine French cuisine. Centennial
building with a cordial ambiance.
Table d'hôte offered during lunch
includes an entrée, a main dish, a
dessert and a coffee.

VENTS DU SUD
323 Roy East, Plateau
(514) 281-9913
Market-style cuisine offering a
traditional French menu.
Generous portions. Ideal for the
customers who like homemade
cooking. Divided into two rooms.

LAVAL & NORTH SHORE

ACADÉMIE (L')
1730 Pierre Péladeau, Laval
(450) 988-1015
French and Italian cuisine.
Welcoming ambiance. Table
d'hôte during lunch and dinner
that includes soup, salad, main
dish and coffee. Affordable price.
Bring your own wine.

ANCESTRAL (L')
625 St. Martin West, Laval
(450) 662-1117
An early 19th century house
converted into a restaurant.
French and Mediterranean
cuisine. Friendly ambiance.
Capacity of 225 clients, including
a reception room. Catering
services available.

BINIOU (AU)
100 Blvd. de la Concorde
East, Laval
(450) 667-3170
Fine cuisine. Menu composed of
game meats, offals, lamb, veal
and other specialties. Table
d'hôte with five services. Rustic
ambiance. Includes a reception
room.

ESCARGOT FOU (L')

5303 Blvd. Lévesque, Laval
(450) 664-3105
Restaurant specializing in
mussels. Cordial ambiance spread
out on two floors. Includes a
reception room of 50 places.
Bring your own wine.

FOLICHON (LE)

804 St. François Xavier,
Terrebonne
(450) 492-1863
Restaurant located in a house
dating from the 19th century.
Diversified menu: rognons, duck
liver, seafood, etc. Cordial and
quiet ambiance with a fireplace.
On two floors with a 70 seat
terrasse.

MENUS-PLAISIRS (LES)

244 Blvd. St. Rose, Laval
(450) 625-0976
Gastronomy focused in game
meats and ostrich. Menu à la
carte and table d'hôte offered
during lunch and dinner. Open for
lunch 5 days a week and open for
dinner every night. Warm
atmosphere.

PLOGONNEC (LE)

1 Blvd. St. Rose, Laval
(450) 625-1510
Fine French cuisine. Intimate and
romantic dining room heated with
a fireplace. Seats 40. Closed for
lunch.

SIRÈNE (LA)

480 St. Martin West, Laval
(450) 662-1999
Reception rooms for all
occasions: seven rooms for 30 to
200 people. Specialties: Italian
dishes, grilled meats and French
cuisine.

TROU NORMAND (AU)

110 rte. 117, Laval
(450) 246-3917
Family atmosphere. Restaurant of
50 places. Beautiful decor. French
cuisine specializing in grilled
meats.

VIEILLE HISTOIRE (LA)

284 Blvd. St. Rose, Laval
(450) 625-0379
French cuisine with a menu that
changes each season. Bring your
own wine. Good selection of
game meats and meat offals.
Serene atmosphere. Two rooms:
one with 20 seats and another of
40 seats. Interior court. Open
every day starting at 6 pm.

SOUTH SHORE

AUBERGE LES CIGALES

585 Victoria, St. Lambert
(450) 466-2197
Restaurant located in a 100-year-
old house. French cuisine with a
good selection of red and white
meats, offals (rice with veal and
veal kidneys). Capacity of 60
clients. Cordial and intimate
ambiance. Modern decor.

CHEZ JULIEN

130 ch. de St. Jean, La Prairie
(450) 659-1678
Bistro restaurant of 64 places.
Daily specials. Table d'hôte that
changes at lunch and dinner, with
12 to 14 choice each day. Casual
atmosphere with jazz music.

CÔTE à CÔTE (LE)

12 St. Mathieu, Beloeil
(450) 464-1633
Cuisine specializing in grilled
meats and seafood. Cordial and
intimate ambiance. Specials
available occasionally. Capacity of
60 clients with a large terrasse of
about a hundred places.

IMPRÉVU (L')

163 St. Jacques,
St. Jean sur Richelieu
(450) 346-2417
Fine French cuisine with a varied
menu: seafood, offals and
prepared dishes. Casual
ambiance. Capacity of 100 with a
terrasse of 60 seats.

JOZÉPHIL (LE)

969 Richelieu, Beloeil
(450) 446-9751
Fine French cuisine. Table d'hôte
offered during lunch and dinner.
Intimate and rustic ambiance and
decor. Beautiful terrasse with a
view of the Richelieu and Mont
St. Hilaire. Capacity of 45.

LOU NISSART

260 St. Jean, Longueuil
(450) 442-2499
Cuisine from the south of France
at an affordable price. Pleasant
and animated ambiance. Table
d'hôte offered during lunch and
dinner.

MAISON BLEUE (LA)

2592 Bourgogne , Montérégie
(450) 447-1112
House dating back to 1815.
Specialties: game meats, seafood
and a great selection of offals.
Large open terrasse and a closed
terrasse under a top. Reception
room. Calm ambiance. Brunch on
Sundays. Children under six eat
for free.

MAISON VERTE (LA)

16981 Blvd. Gouin West,
Montérégie
(514) 696-6308
Fine market-style cuisine
specializing in game meats.
Romantic ambiance and private
room with a fireplace.

OSTERIA DU VIEUX BELOEIL

914 Laurier, Beloeil
(450) 464-7491
French and Italian cuisine.
Specialties include game meats,
fresh fish, pasta and cutlets. One
of the most beautiful wine cellars
in the area.

RELAIS TERRAPIN (LE)

295 St. Charles West,
Longueuil
(450) 677-6378
French and continental cuisine.
Try their steak Diane flamed
with cognac. The decor is
complimented with rustic
woodwork. Cordial and friendly
ambiance. Breakfast served from
7:30 am to 11 am. Open for over
21 years. Centennial building
(1853).

SARCELLES (LES)

1031 Victoria, St. Lambert
(450) 671-0946
French cuisine with a taste of
the country specializing in duck.
Establishment with several
rooms: antique, with fireplace,
private room with couch and
armchair. Reception room can
accommodate 40 patrons.

SAULAIE (LA)

1161 rte. Marie-Victorin,
Boucherville
(450) 449-5005
Restaurant of fine French and
continental cuisine on the bank of
the St. Lawrence River. Cordial
ambiance. Menu à la carte
featuring something for every
pallet. Reception room with a
fireplace which can accommodate
55 clients. Good value.

SAMUEL II

291 Richelieu,
St. Jean sur Richelieu
(450) 347-4353
Fine French cuisine. High quality
dining room. The large windows
offer a splendid view of the river.
Specialty: house smoked salmon.
Romantic ambiance. Table d'hôte
is half price during lunch.

VIEUX FORT (AU)

120 ch. de St. Jean, La Prairie
(450) 444-4346
Ancestral house converted into a
restaurant where one can enjoy
good French cuisine at an
affordable price.

VRAI CHABLIS (LE)

52 Aberdeen, St. Lambert
(450) 465-2795
Home-style French cuisine. Family
ambiance. Table d'hôte offered
during lunch and dinner for a
price varying between $15 to
$30, which includes entrée, soup,
main dish, dessert and coffee.

ⓢ *Fusion*

ANUBIS

35 Mount Royal East, Plateau
(514) 843-3391
Restaurant with an inviting and
beautiful ambiance and a
harmonious decor. Possibility of
reservation for parties and for big
groups.

AREA
1429 Amherst, East End
(514) 890-6691
Refined and casual restaurant. Different menu every three months. Affordable prices. For the daring: a special sampling menu at $50.

SAVANNAH
4448 St. Laurent Blvd. (St. Lawrence), Plateau
(514) 904-0277
Louisiana-style cuisine with African and European influences. Their salmon tartare is a must. Unique cuisine in Montreal. Varied menu.

© *German*

BERLIN
101 Fairmount West, Plateau
(514) 270-3000
Authentic German cuisine. Beautiful ambiance during the week; beer garden atmosphere on weekends. Table d'hôte from Sunday to Thursday. Musicians on occasions. Seats 85.

© *Greek*

ISLAND OF MONTREAL

CABANE GRECQUE
102 Prince Arthur East, Plateau
(514) 849-0122
Large, two-floor Greek restaurant. Higher quality but at a reasonable price. Excellent seafood. Bring your own wine.

CASA GRECQUE
200 Prince Arthur East, Plateau
(514) 842-6098
Excellent place for eating well at a moderate price. Table d'hôte starting at $15. Lunch menu for as little as $5. Children eat for free from Sunday to Thursday. Mediterranean dishes that will keep you coming back for more! Bring your own wine.

CASA GRECQUE
3855-A, St. John's Blvd., West Island
(514) 626-6626

CASA GRECQUE
5787 Sherbrooke St. East, East End
(514) 899-5373

CASA GRECQUE
7218 Blvd. Newman, South End
(514) 364-0494
See also Laval & North Shore and South Shore

CAVERNE GRECQUE
105 Prince Arthur East, Plateau
(514) 844-5114
Great establishment on two floors. Up-to-date Greek cuisine of higher quality. Specialties: brochettes, steaks and seafood. Bring your own wine.

GOURMET GREC

180 Prince Arthur East,
Plateau
(514) 849-1335
Specializing in authentic Greek
cuisine and seafood. Dishes start
for as little as $7 and go up to
$25. Bring your own wine.

HERMES

1014 Jean Talon West,
North End
(514) 272-3880
Authentic Greek restaurant with
historical decorations. Capacity
of 150. A Greek antiquity
ambiance.

JARDIN DE PANOS

521 Duluth East, Plateau
(514) 521-4206
Charming restaurant specializing
in brochettes and moderately
priced seafood. Typical Greek
decor. Bring your own wine.

JARDIN DE PUITS

180 Villeneuve East, Plateau
(514) 849-0555
Quality menu at a reasonable
price. Summer terrasse with a
capacity of 120 people. Cordial
ambiance.

MAISON GRECQUE

450 Duluth East, Plateau
(514) 842-0969
Open for over 22 years. Several
Greek entrées with a diversity of
seafood, steaks and brochettes.

MARVEN

880 Ball, North End
(514) 277-3625
Greek restaurant of good quality
at a respectable price. Varied
menu: calamari, steaks, souvlakis.
Seats 110 clients.

NEW TRIPOLIS

679 St. Roch, North End
(514) 277-4689
Small charming restaurant of 60
places, ideal for outings between
friends or with family. Authentic
Greek cuisine specializing in
seafood and grilled meats. High
quality ingredients. Extraordinary
octopus. Open 24 hours.

OUZÉRI

4690 St. Denis, Plateau
(514) 845-1336
Traditional cuisine. Specializing in
lamb with tzatziki and octopus.
Fast service and a great selection
of wine. Simple and friendly!

PREMIÈRE (LA)

4622 Verdun, South End
(514) 767-6760
Greek restaurant whose menu
offers a great choice of dishes:
souvlakis, seafood, brochettes.
Modern and casual ambiance.

PRINCE ARTHUR (LE)

54 Prince Arthur East, Plateau
(514) 849-2454
Greek cuisine specializing in
brochettes and seafood. Dishes
are between $8 and $30. Try

their prawns, an out of the ordinary delight.

PSAROTAVERNA DU SYMPOSIUM

3829 St. Denis, Plateau
(514) 842-0867
Specializing in cuisine from the Greek islands. Large variety of fresh fish and seafood. Terrasse for 20 people in the summer.

PSAROTAVERNA DU SYMPOSIUM

5334 Park Ave., Plateau
(514) 274-7022

Laval & North Shore

CASA GRECQUE

1565 Daniel Johnson, Laval
(450) 663-1031
Excellent place for eating well at a moderate price. Table d'hôte starting at $15. Lunch menu for as little as $5. Children eat for free from Sunday to Thursday. Mediterranean dishes that will keep you coming back for more! Bring your own wine.

CASA GRECQUE

259 Blvd. Labelle, St. Thérèse
(450) 979-4619

CASA GRECQUE

574 Blvd. Arthur Sauvé, Laval
(450) 974-2929

CASA GRECQUE

852 Blvd. des Seigneurs, Laval
(450) 492-2888

South Shore

CASA GRECQUE

690 de Montbrun, Boucherville
(450) 449-2249
Excellent place for eating well at a moderate price. Table d'hôte starting at $15. Lunch menu for as little as $5. Children eat for free from Sunday to Thursday. Mediterranean dishes that will keep you comingback for more! Bring your own wine.

CASA GRECQUE

8245-A, Taschereau Blvd., Brossard
(450) 443-0323

CASA GRECQUE

3094 ch. de Chambly, Longueuil
(450) 646-2228

◎ *Grill*

Laval & North Shore

MEZZANINA (LA)

2515 Blvd. Le Corbusier, Laval
(450) 688-5515
Specialties: Italian seafood and grilled meats. Modern decor with orchestra on Fridays and Saturdays.

🌀 *Indian*

ALLÔ INDE
1422 Stanley, Downtown
(514) 288-7878
Fine cuisine with a sublime presentation. Indian ambiance and an impeccable service. Vast choice in the menu à la carte. Delivery service available.

AMBALA
3887 St. Denis, Plateau
(514) 499-0446
Fine Indian cuisine. Lunch dishes for as low as $6. Specialties: butter chicken and tandoori.

ASHA
3490 Park Ave., Plateau
(514) 844-3178
Authentic Indian cuisine: goat, lamb, chicken, etc. Great selection of spicy dishes at a handsome price.

BOMBAY PALACE
2201 St. Catherine St. West, Downtown
(514) 932-7141
Classic Indian restaurant and buffet. Selection of dishes from all corners of India, including Kashmir. Their butter chicken is a must. Modern decor and professional service.

BOMBAY PALACE
3343 Sources Blvd., West Island
(514) 685-7777

GANDHI
230 St. Paul West, Old Montreal
(514) 845-5866
Chic Indian restaurant with an elegant decor and a refined cuisine. Presentation made with care. The menu includes all the traditional dishes.

INDIA BEAU VILLAGE
752 Jarry West, North End
(514) 272-5847
Very reasonably priced Indian cuisine, specializing in pakoras, samosas, tikka and tandoori. Simple menu without pretension.

INDIRA
4295 St. Denis, Plateau
(514) 848-0838
North-west Indian cuisine. Lunch special: vegetarian and meat dishes for two. Sliding doors open during the summer. Delivery service available for a minimum order of $7.

LUNE INDIENNE (LA)
2018 St. Denis, Downtown
(514) 281-1402
Cordial, small Indian restaurant specializing in tandoori. Table d'hôte offered every evening.

MAISON DE CARI GOLDEN

5210 St. Laurent Blvd.
(St. Lawrence), Plateau
(514) 270-2561
Small authentic Indian restaurant.
Food prepared with care.
Excellent Dhansak beef and
spinach lamb.

NOUVEAU DELHI

3464 St. Denis, Plateau
(514) 845-7977
Indian restaurant at a moderate
price. Tables d'hôtes with five
dishes starting at $11. Traditional
dishes. Moderately spiced meals,
but you can ask for more
seasoning. Sliding doors open
during the summer. Try their
Indian beer.

PALAIS DE L'INDE

5125 St. Laurent Blvd.
(St. Lawrence), Plateau
(514) 270-7402
Fine Indian cuisine at a
reasonable price. Excellent
Tandoori chicken with Naan
bread. Large variety of dishes
and an elegant ambiance.

ROYAL CARI

5215 St. Laurent Blvd.
(St. Lawrence), Plateau
(514) 278-8211
Authentic cuisine with a menu
comprised of all your favourite
Indian dishes. Restaurant with a
bar; traditional decor. Capacity of
60. Open for over 12 years. It is
preferable to reserve for Fridays
and Saturdays. Delivery service
with a minimum order of $15.

SHED TANDOORI

4886A Sources Blvd.,
West Island
(514) 683-8737
Authentic cuisine at an affordable
price. Menu à la carte and table
d'hôte offered for lunch and
dinner. Famous restaurant for its
fine cuisine and its decor.
Capacity of 50 clients with a
terrasse.

SHEZAN

2051 St. Denis, Downtown
(514) 845-8867
Small Indian restaurant of
60 places. Intimate and family
ambiance. Menu and table d'hôte
offered. Delivery. All dishes are
less expensive when one eats on
location.

SITAR

4961D Queen Mary,
Mount Royal
(514) 735-9801
Elegant and cordial restaurant
with a serene atmosphere. Fine
Indian cuisine. Try their onion
bhajia. Lunch specials. Open for
over 16 years. Special events
upon request.

SUNAM TANDOORI

1334 Van Horne,
Mount Royal
(514) 272-2045
Authentic Indian restaurant.
Lunch menu is served between

11:30 am and 2:30 pm. Specials for as little as $8. Delivery possible with orders of over $15.

TAJ (LE)

2077 Stanley, Downtown
(514) 845-9015
Authentic restaurant with a bar and buffet during lunch. Ventilated space and a casual ambiance with a modern and traditional decor. Beautiful view of their naan bread oven.

TAJ MAHAL DE L'OUEST

5026 Sherbrooke St. West, West End
(514) 482-0076
Traditional Indian restaurant. Specialties: tandoori and vegetarian dishes. English draft beer.

ÉTOILE DES INDES

1806 St. Catherine St. West, Downtown
(514) 932-8330
Authentic Indian restaurant. Varied menu representing all the corners of India. Two floors.

◎ *International*

ISLAND OF MONTREAL

AMBIANCE

1874 Notre Dame West, South End
(514) 939-2609
International bistro cuisine. Specializing in sandwiches, salads, steaks and seafood. Open only during the day; evenings are reserved for groups. Decorated with antiques.

BONNE CARTE (LA)

1 du Casino, Old Montreal
(514) 392-2709
Restaurant with a buffet. Located in the Casino. Menu à la carte also available. Specialties: steaks, seafood and buffet. During the day the buffet is $13.50 and during the evening it's $18.95. Save money on the buffet by getting the 'Privilege' card. Chic and cordial decor.

BOULEVARD (LE)

1201 Blvd. René Lévesque (fka Dorchester) West, Downtown
(514) 878-2000
Restaurant with a table d'hôte and lunch buffet for $15. Menu à la carte in the evenings. Reception room: call to reserve. Elegant style. Open for over 20 years. Inside the Sheraton.

CAFÉ NICOLE

1180 Mountain (de la Montagne), Downtown
(514) 861-6000
Restaurant located in the Novotel Hotel. Specialties: fish, meats and sandwiches. Table d'hôte offered during lunch and dinner. Capacity of 60 clients. Breakfast, buffet and menu à la carte. Modern decor.

CAFÉ ST-PAUL

143 St. Paul West, Old
Montreal

(514) 844-7225

Cuisine specializing in Quebec
dishes: 'pâté chinois', meat pie,
etc. Breakfast à la carte; table
d'hôte available for lunch and
dinner. Rustic decor with vines.
Open every day. Delivery service
available.

CASEY'S RESTO-BAR

1001 Victoria Square,
Old Montreal

(514) 875-9969

Restaurant bar and grill.
Specialties: fajitas and filet
mignon. Excellent environment
for family and friends.

CASEY'S RESTO-BAR

1031 du Marché Central,
North End

(514) 382-1234

CLAREMONT

5032 Sherbrooke St. West,
West End

(514) 483-1557

Restaurant with a casual and
relaxed style - not too chic. A
large variety of international
dishes. Try their calamari and
their dumplings.

CLUB DU VILLAGE (LE)

4 Somerville, West End

(514) 485-2502

Restaurant specializing in duck
and rack of lamb. Cordial
ambiance ideal for couples.

Capacity of 40 clients. It is
preferable to reserve. Open only
for dinner.

CÉPAGE (AU)

212 Notre Dame West

(514) 845-5436

Contemporary bistro with a
diversified menu: French, Italian,
Indian, Spanish, etc, cuisine.
Personalized menu. Beautiful
ambiance with a bar and a
terrasse. Several rooms. Ideal for
parties.

DEUX CHEFS (LES)

2876 Masson, North End

(514) 725-2015

French gastronomy influenced by
Mediterranean and Caribbean
cuisine - New World-style.
Eclectic, intimate and romantic
ambiance.

FLAMBERGE (LA)

5600 Blvd. Henri Bourassa
East, North End

(514) 852-0642

Varied cuisine with numerous
specialties. Table d'hôte offered
at lunch and dinner, which
changes each day. Wine, beer and
spirits. Cordial ambiance with a
beautiful decor. Capacity of 190
clients. Reception room and
delivery service available.

JARDINS LE PAVILLON

7700 aut. de la Côte de
Liesse, North End

(514) 731-7821

Restaurant of fine international
cuisine. Gourmet menu and table

d'hôte offered during lunch and dinner. Buffet served for breakfast. Capacity of 75. Inside a hotel.

TERRASSE LAFAYETTE
250 Villeneuve West, Plateau
(514) 288-3915
Cordial ambiance with a summer terrasse. Large variety: French, Canadian, Italian and Greek cuisine. Buy three small pizzas and the fourth one is free. Bring your own wine.

TULIPE NOIRE (LA)
7655 Decarie Blvd.,
Mount Royal
(514) 735-2233
Open for over 15 years. Specializing in salads and sandwiches. Recognized for their pasta and homemade desserts. Varied menu with breakfasts. Perfect ambiance for the family. Delivery service available.

UPSTAIRS JAZZ CLUB & RESTO
1254 Mackay, Downtown
(514) 931-6808
Menu with several specialties: beefsteak of ribs, lamb, grilled salmon, mahi mahi and calamari. Elegant ambiance with a small grand piano and an aquarium; in short, ideal for couples. Musicians playing every day during the winter and from Monday to Thursday during the summer. Excellent wine list.

SOUTH SHORE

CASEY'S RESTO-BAR
1165 Volta, Boucherville
(450) 641-4800
Restaurant bar and grill. Specialties: fajitas and filet mignon. Excellent environment for family friends.

CASEY'S RESTO-BAR
7400 Taschereau Blvd.,
Brossard
(450) 466-6809

St. MATHIEU (LE)
80 St. Mathieu, Beloeil
(450) 536-0604
Modern cuisine, specializing in the various flavours from around the world. New England-style decor.

© *Irish*

HURLEY'S
1225 Crescent, Downtown
(514) 861-4111
Restaurant-bar with terrasse, specializing in imported beers. Animated and cordial place; typical Irish ambiance.

MCKIBBIN'S
1426 Bishop, Downtown
(514) 288-1580
Great establishment of three floors with a pub, restaurant and discotheque. Menu à la carte with a happy hour from 5 pm to 8 pm, Monday to Friday. Musicians every day. Quiz night on Mondays

with prizes to be won. Irish ambiance.

◎ *Italian*

ISLAND OF MONTREAL

AL CAPRICCIO
1506 Blvd. St. Jean-Baptiste, East End
(514) 645-1001
Restaurant of fine Italian cuisine. Children's menu. Dancing on Fridays and Saturdays. Reception room for 70 people.

AL DENTE
5768 Monkland, West End
(514) 486-4343
Italian home-style restaurant. Wood oven, fresh pasta, 30 different sauces. Typical decor of Italian trattorias.

AMALFITANA (L')
1381 Blvd. René Lévesque (fka Dorchester) East, East End
(514) 523-2483
Fine Italian cuisine. Romantic and calm ambiance with a beautiful canopy. Specialties: pescatore linguini and vitello amalfi. Table d'hôte offered during lunch and dinner.

ANTICO MARTINI
6450 Somerled, West End
(514) 489-6804
Traditional Italian restaurant with a very good ambiance. Excellent service and a great selection of dishes at various prices.

ANTINORI RISTORANTE
617 Decarie Blvd., North End
(514) 748-2202
Refined Italian cuisine. Lunch table d'hôte starting at $13. Evening menu starting at $16. Good selection of dishes: seafood, pasta, grilled meats and lamb.

BELLAGIO RISTORANTE
505 de Maisonneuve West, Downtown
(514) 845-9505
Large family restaurant specializing in Mediterranean cuisine. Lunch special includes an entrée, coffee and dessert. At night, choice between a shrimp plate, lamb or filet mignon.

BUENA SERA
4701 St. John's Blvd., West Island
(514) 624-0466
Italian family restaurant at an affordable price. Varied menu, wood oven. Table d'hôte offered during lunch and dinner. Reception room for big groups.

BUONA FORCHETTA (LA)
2407 Mount Royal East, Plateau
(514) 521-6766
Romantic Italian restaurant with central fireplace. Fine home-style cuisine. Table d'hôte served during lunch and dinner. Capacity of 90 clients with a private room of 45 places. Cellar with 450 kinds of wines: 4,000 bottles in all.

BUONA NOTTE

3518 St. Laurent Blvd. (St. Lawrence), Plateau
(514) 848-0644
Modern Italian restaurant. Homemade pasta, table d'hôte offered every day and always fresh fish. Music with a DJ.

CAFFE EPOCA

6778 St. Laurent Blvd. (St. Lawrence), Mount Royal
(514) 276-6569
Charming Italian restaurant. Simple and tasty cuisine. Table d'hôte offered during lunch. Animated ambiance, especially during big events like hockey games.

CAFÉ TERRASSE GILDONE

9700 Blvd. St. Michel, North End
(514) 389-6732
Small rustic cafe of 30 places. Choice between three types of pastas; cuisine specialized in mushrooms.

CAFÉ VIA DANTE

251 Dante, Mount Royal
(514) 270-8446
Charming Italian cafe. Casual and cordial ambiance, like in Italy. Different menu each day. Excellent cuisine. Seafood, pasta, etc. Good variety.

CANTINA (LA)

9090 St. Laurent Blvd. (St. Lawrence), North End
(514) 382-3618
Relaxed atmosphere with a typical Mediterranean-style hospitality. Table d'hôte offered during lunch and dinner. Great selection of dishes: pasta, game meats, seafood, grilled meats, veal scallopine. Fresh products. Great wine selection.

CAPANNINA (LA)

2022 Stanley, Downtown
(514) 845-1852
Fine cuisine specializing in pastas and veal. Elegant ambiance with a modern decor. Table d'hôte includes an entrée, main dish, coffee and dessert. Capacity of 110 clients.

CARISSIMA TRATTORIA

222 Mount Royal East, Plateau
(514) 844-7283
Cordial restaurant with a fireplace. Supper with show. Table d'hôte during lunch is between $7 and $13 and during dinner between $12 and $22. Great selection of dishes: pastas, pizzas, duck, veal, seafood, grilled meats.

CASA CACCIATORE

170 Jean Talon East, Mount Royal
(514) 274-1240
Cordial restaurant with an antique decor. Home-style cuisine; fresh

homemade pasta. Varied menu. Evening table d'hôte is between $22 and $35. Great wine selection.

CASA NAPOLI

6728 St. Laurent Blvd. (St. Lawrence), Mount Royal
(514) 274-4351
Fine Italian cuisine with a bistro. Specialties: sorrentinas crêpes, veal, seafood.

CHEZ ENNIO

1978 de Maisonneuve West, West End
(514) 933-8168
Small restaurant, home-style cuisine. Perfect for romantic dinners. Table d'hôte with three choices of meat. Bring your own wine.

CHEZ PAESANO

1669 St. Denis, Downtown
(514) 982-6638
Restaurant of fine Italian cuisine. Specialties: veal, fresh hand made pasta, seafood, grilled meats. Very casual ambiance; candlelight dinner.

CIOCIARA (LA)

7681 Blvd. Newman, South End
(514) 366-8896
Pleasant, typical Italian ambiance. Choices between pasta, veal, fish and seafood. Lunch table d'hôte between $14 and $18. Dinner table d'hôte between $17 and $23.

CUCINA LINDA RISTORANTE

3900 Wellington, South End
(514) 362-9618
Traditional restaurant. Great selection of dishes: pasta, veal, chicken. Table d'hôte includes five choices of soup, entrées and main dish. Music on weekends.

D'AMICHI

25 Blvd. Bishop Power, South End
(514) 595-9199
Family restaurant that won several awards. Splendid view of the rapids and large open terrasse in the summer. Varied menu: pasta, seafood, meats. Table d'hôte offered all week.

DA ATTILIO

5282 St. Laurent Blvd. (St. Lawrence), Plateau
(514) 274-8447
Italian restaurant with a cordial ambiance. Fine authentic Roman-style cuisine. Specialties: pastas, veal and seafood. Table d'hôte offered during lunch and dinner.

DA EMMA

777 de la Commune West, Old Montreal
(514) 392-1568
Beautiful romantic restaurant of fine Roman cuisine. Specialties: pasta, meats of great quality and seafood. Capacity of 160 clients.

DA MARCELLO

1251 Gilford, Plateau
(514) 524-3812

Fine Tuscan cuisine. Romantic ambiance with a summer terrasse. Table d'hôte changes each day. Sampling menu and menu à la carte include homemade pasta and seafood. Reception room.

DEL VERDE

1289 Laird, Mount Royal
(514) 342-2166

Chic restaurant of fine cuisine. Table d'hôte offered during lunch and dinner. Specialties: veal, fish, pasta, seafood. Private room. Great wine selection.

DI LUSSO

2351 Jean Talon East,
North End
(514) 376-0281

Menu includes fresh pasta, meats, fish and various antipasti. Elegant decor. Always fresh ingredients. Fast and knowledgeable service. It is preferable to reserve.

DI MENNA

6313 Jarry East, East End
(514) 326-4200

Fine Italian cuisine. European decor. Romantic ambiance with a fireplace. Table d'hôte during lunch and dinner includes an entrée, main dish, coffee and dessert.

DIVA (LA)

1273 Blvd. René Lévesque
(fka Dorchester) East,
Downtown
(514) 523-3470

Small Italian restaurant with a terrasse. Authentic and sublime cuisine. Fresh ingredients prepared with meticulousness. Table d'hôte offered during lunch and dinner. Large variety of dishes. Specialty of the house: veal liver with onions.

DORA (LA)

6837 Sherbrooke St. East,
East End
(514) 255-8841

Cordial and typical Italian ambiance. Varied menu; the meat is excellent. Children's menu. The daily special includes an entrée, a main dish and a dessert.

EAST SIDE MARIO'S

3131 ch. de la Côte-Vertu,
North End
(514) 331-7172

American-Italian cuisine in the style of New York's Little Italy. Family ambiance; New-York decor. Menu includes pizzas, pastas, grilled chicken, salads, mussels and hamburgers.

EAST SIDE MARIO'S

3237 Sources Blvd.,
West Island
(514) 421-6551

EAST SIDE MARIO'S
4485 Jean Talon East,
East End
(514) 727-8848

EMILIO'S CAFÉ
4705 Sources Blvd.,
West Island
(514) 683-0011
Three star restaurant. Very
modern, beautiful decor. Large
variety of dishes: veal, lamb,
chicken, pizzas and pastas. Table
d'hôte offered during lunch
and dinner.

EUGENIO
350 de Liège East, North End
(514) 858-6030
Fine cuisine. Specialties:
homemade pasta and seafood.
Table d'hôte offered during lunch
and dinner. Romantic and casual
ambiance. Capacity of 70 clients.

EVOLUZIONE
3458 Park Ave, Plateau
(514) 499-6999
Fine Italian Cuisine. Brick decor.
Accepts all major credit cards.

FERRARI
1407 Bishop, Downtown
(514) 843-3086
Restaurant-bistro with a cordial
ambiance, perfect for business
people. Specialty: homemade
pasta. Table d'hôte offered during
lunch and dinner. Large terrasse
during the summer.

FINNEGAN & BACCHUS
1458 Mountain (de la
Montagne), Downtown
(514) 842-8825
Huge restaurant of 700 places
specializing in fine Italian and
French cuisine. Menu à la carte
only. Beautiful ambiance with a
bar and a club with exotic
dancers.

FOCCACIA DI CARPACCIO
2077 University, Downtown
(514) 284-1115
Fine cuisine specializing in
homemade pasta. Menu à la carte
and buffet from 5 pm to 7 pm.
Restaurant-bar ambiance with a
terrasse and from time to time,
live music.

FONTANINA (LA)
3194 St. Joseph, West Island
(514) 637-2475
Serene Italian and French
restaurant. Specials during lunch
and dinner. Varied menu: pasta,
veal, fish and seafood. Reception
room for 50 clients.

FORNARINA (LA)
6825 St. Laurent Blvd.
(St. Lawrence), Mount Royal
(514) 271-1741
Family atmosphere with a
reception room for 30 to 70
people. Specializing in pizzas
cooked in a wood oven. Table
d'hôte offered only during lunch.
Bring your own wine.

FOUR DE ST- LÉONARD (LE)
7605 Blvd. Lacordaire,
East End
(514) 374-3687
Restaurant with an incredible quality/price value. Rustic decor. Table d'hôte offered every day and all you can eat oysters on Wednesdays. Pizzas are cooked in a wood oven, pastas al dente, large selection of renowned wines. Always fresh ingredients.

FRANK
65 St. Zotique East, Mount Royal (514) 273-7734
Traditional Italian restaurant, casual atmosphere. Lunch table d'hôte between $18 and $38. In the evening, the table d'hôte is between $24 and $38. Specialties: pasta, seafood and game meats.

GALLIANO'S
410 St. Vincent, Old Montreal
(514) 861-5039
Authentic cuisine, excellent price for the quality. Superb ambiance, perfect for big groups or special events. Table d'hôte offered during lunch and dinner. Sublime veal scallopine, just like all the items on the menu.

GIOCONDA (LA)
5625 Decarie Blvd.,
Mount Royal
(514) 731-1109
Fine home-style cuisine. Modern and very cordial ambiance. Great selection of dishes: pastas, pizzas, seafood. Menu à la carte only.

GIORGIO
200 St. Laurent Blvd.
(St. Lawrence), Old Montreal
(514) 845-4221
Italian restaurant. Excellent cuisine at low prices. Great for family outings. Courteous and fast service. Table d'hôte includes soup, main dish, coffee and dessert. Specialties: pastas, pizzas, veal and chicken with sauce.

GIORGIO
10350 Blvd. Pie-IX, East End
(514) 323-9704

GIORGIO
12585 Sherbrooke St. East,
East End
(514) 645-2002

GIORGIO
5955 Blvd. Gouin West,
North End
(514) 745-1313

GIORGIO
6130 Blvd. Louis-Hippolyte-Lafontaine, East End
(514) 352-1144

GIORGIO
6675 Jean Talon East, East End
(514) 252-1916

HOSTARIA ROMANA
2044 Metcalfe, Downtown
(514) 849-1389
Restaurant of fine Italian cuisine, open for over 25 years. Table d'hôte offered during lunch and diner includes an entrée, main dish, salad and dessert. Musicians on Fridays.

IL BOCCALINI
1408 de l'Église, North End
(514) 747-7809
Fine Italian and Mediterranean cuisine. Very elegant Mediterranean decor. Beautiful open terrasse during the summer. Specialties: Italian and Mediterranean swordfish. Menu includes grilled meats, veal, pastas, pizzas and seafood. Table d'hôte every evening starting at $23.

IL BONGUSTO
150 Jean Talon East, Mount Royal
(514) 274-1015
Superb Italian cuisine. Remarkable value for money. Sober and discrete decor. Pasta dishes start at $11 and the table d'hôte starts at $20. Great selection of dishes. Experienced service.

IL CAVALIERE
1199 Berri, Downtown
(514) 845-9968
Charming romantic restaurant. Specialties: veal and pastas. Lunch and dinner table d'hôte.

Breakfast served between 7 am and 11:30 am. Three reception rooms, capacity between 25 and 80 people.

IL FOCALAIO
1223 Phillips Square, Downtown
(514) 879-1045
Traditional restaurant specializing in pizzas. Choice between 70 kinds of the best pizzas in town, all cooked in a wood oven. Buy four pizzas for delivery and the fifth one is free.

IL FORNETTO
1900 St. Joseph, West Island
(514) 637-5253
Large restaurant of fine Italian cuisine specializing in pasta, pizzas and seafood. Table d'hôte offered during lunch and dinner. Terrasse is situated right next to the St. Louis canal. Very cordial.

IL GALATEO
5315 Gatineau, Mount Royal
(514) 737-1606
Renowned, fine Italian cuisine. Very cordial and chic. Table d'hôte and menu.

IL MARE
2487 Rachel East, Plateau
(514) 529-7898
Small family restaurant specializing in fine home-style cuisine. Everthing is made on location. Choices between four dishes each day that include fruits, nuts, house biscuits, coffee, tiramisu and a shooter

after dinner. Open on Friday and Saturdays evenings. The remainder of the week operates only through reservations.

IL PAZZESCO

7031 Jarry East, East End
(514) 353-3801
Two separated rooms, for smokers and nonsmokers. A guitar player during the weekends: soft music. Capacity of 110 clients.

IL PIATTO DELLA NONNA

176 St. Viateur West, Plateau
(514) 278-6066
Authentic Italian cuisine with a beautiful open kitchen. Specialties of the house: sauces, homemade pasta always cooked al dente and osso bucco. Good Italian wine selection. Personalized ambiance.

IL POSTO

9030 de l'Acadie, North End
(514) 850-0000
Fine Italian cuisine. Relaxed ambiance. Table d'hôte offered during lunch and dinner. Various promotions every day. Reception room available.

IL PUNTINO

7751 Blvd. Roi-René,
North End
(514) 355-6213
Small restaurant of fine cuisine. Cordial ambiance. Table d'hôte during lunch and dinner. Always fresh pasta. Excellent wine list.

IL SOLE

3627 St. Laurent Blvd.
(St. Lawrence), Plateau
(514) 282-4996
Fine regional Italian cuisine. Specialty: homemade pasta. Italian bistro ambiance. Open only at night. Select wine list.

LA TRATTORIA

5563 Upper Lachine Road
(514) 484-5303   *$15 to $30*
Far from Little Italy but a wonderful Italian restaurant. Fine selection of pasta in a wine cellar atmosphere. Bring your own wine.

LA TRATTORIA

1551 Notre Dame West
(514) 935-5050   *$15 to $30*

LOMBARDI

411 Duluth East, Plateau
(514) 844-9419
Fine cuisine specializing in homemade pasta, seafood and meats. Table d'hôte offered during lunch and dinner. Caring staff. Bring your own wine.

MARCO

82 St. Anne, West Island
(514) 457-3850
Large Italian and Greek restaurant specializing in pizzas and other Mediterranean dishes. Table d'hôte offered during lunch and dinner includes coffee and soup. Terrasse with a beautiful view of the river.

MEDUSA (LA)

1224 Drummond, Downtown
(514) 878-4499
Small intimate restaurant of 45 places. Fine Italian cuisine specializing in homemade pasta, seafood and veal. Table d'hôte offered during lunch and dinner.

MEZZOGIORNO

3565 Blvd. St. Charles, West Island
(514) 426-9288
Traditional Italian restaurant with a plush ambiance. Specializing in veal. Table d'hôte offered during lunch starting at $11 and during dinner starting at $20.

MINERVA

17 Prince Arthur East, Plateau
(514) 842-5451
Menu composed of Italian, Greek and seafood dishes. Romantic ambiance. Table d'hôte offered during lunch and dinner. Capacity of 500 clients.

MIRRA

252 Lakeshore (Bord du Lac), West Island
(514) 695-6222
Fine cuisine. Romantic decor. Table d'hôte offered during lunch between $15 and $20. During the evening, between $25 and $40. Different table d'hôte each week.

MISTO

929 Mount Royal East, Plateau
(514) 526-5043
Restaurant specializing in pastas and pizzas. Casual atmosphere. Table d'hôte offered during lunch for as little as $8. Excellent wine list.

MOLISANA (LA)

1014 Fleury East, North End
(514) 382-7100
Romantic restaurant specializing in pastas and veal scallopine. Pizzas cooked in a wood oven. Excellent wine list. Reception room for 100 people. Musicians play from Thursday to Sunday.

MUNDO TRATTORIA & MERCANTINO

18425 Antoine-Faucon, West Island
(514) 696-7887
Restaurant of fine Italian cuisine. Rustic decor. Table d'hôte offered during lunch and dinner. Varied menu: pasta, lamb, veal and seafood. Impeccable service. Authentic cuisine.

NAPOLI

1675 St. Denis, Downtown
(514) 845-5905
Home-style cuisine with a vast choice of dishes: pasta, meats and seafood. Rustic Italian ambiance. Table d'hôte includes soup or salad, entrée and a main dish. Two terrasses during the summer.

NATALINO

365 Lakeshore (Bord du Lac),
West Island
(514) 631-5952
Regional Italian cuisine. Table
d'hôte offered during lunch and
dinner. Varied menu. Open for
over 17 years.

PARTICULIER (LE)

2237 Fleury East, North End
(514) 381-0658
Italian and French restaurant.
Romantic ambiance. Capacity of
60 clients. Table d'hôte during
lunch and dinner. Supper with a
blues show on occasion.

PASTA ANDREA

1718 St. Joseph, West Island
(514) 634-3400
Excellent Italian restaurant with a
remarkable value for the money.
Refined cuisine with a table
d'hôte offered during lunch and
dinner which includes several
choices of entrées, main dishes
and desserts. Terrasse with a
beautiful view of the Lachine
canal.

PASTA CASARECCIA

5849 Sherbrooke St. West,
West End
(514) 483-1588
Fine Italian cuisine. Specialty:
homemade pasta. Typical Italian
trattoria decor. Table d'hôte
offered during lunch and dinner.
Great wine selection.

PASTA TELLA

2055 Stanley, Downtown
(514) 842-5344
Italian and Swiss restaurant,
specializing in fresh pastas and
fondues. Table d'hôte offered
during lunch and dinner. Capacity
of 140 with a private room of 40
places and a terrasse.

PAVAROTTI

408 St. François Xavier,
Old Montreal
(514) 844-9656
Small Italian restaurant with an
affordable home-style cuisine.
Impeccable service; plush and
intimate ambiance with fireplace.
Perfect for romantic dinners.
Table d'hôte offered during lunch
and dinner.

PERLA (LA)

6010 Hochelaga, East End
(514) 259-6529
Restaurant of fine Italian cuisine
with a friendly and calm
atmosphere, personalized service.
Serene ambiance. Business
customers during lunch. Table
d'hôte during lunch and dinner.

PETIT ITALIEN (LE)

1265 Bernard West,
Mount Royal
(514) 278-0888
Italian restaurant with a
courteous and fast service. Very
interesting table d'hôte.

PETITE VENISE (LA)

5134 Blvd. Henri Bourassa
East, North End
(514) 321-7307
Fine Italian cuisine; cordial
ambiance. Specializing in pasta,
veal, and seafood. Table d'hôte
offered during lunch and dinner.
Capacity of 70 clients with
possibility of receiving groups of
30 people. Open for over 25
years.

PIANO PIANO

2534 Beaubien East,
North End
(514) 727-7732
Italian and French restaurant.
Calm and relaxed ambiance, with
fireplace. Large variety of dishes:
pizzas, pastas, filet mignon and
pastries. Table d'hôte between
$20 and $25. Close to the
Beaubien cinema.

PIAZZA ROMANA

339 Lakeshore, West Island
(514) 697-3593
Very romantic Italian restaurant.
Great for candlelight dinner. Table
d'hôte offered during lunch and
dinner. Large variety of
homemade pastas. Exceptional
service.

PICCOLO DIAVOLO

1336 St. Catherine St. East,
East End
(514) 526-1336
Casual restaurant with a jazz
ambiance. Specialties: fresh pasta
and grilled meats. Different table

d'hôte each evening. Open for
lunch only on Thursday and
Friday. French doors are opened
during the summer.

PINO

1471 Crescent, Downtown
(514) 289-1930
Fine Italian cuisine with a touch
of fusion. Modern and elegant
decor at this very popular
restaurant. Room with a bar and
fireplace on the second floor.
Ideal for romantic dinners or for
outings between friends.

PRIMA LUNA

7301 Blvd. Henri Bourassa
East, Montreal North
(514) 494-6666
Italian restaurant that also serves
sushi. Modern and elegant.
Traditional Italian dishes. Table
d'hôte offered during lunch and
dinner at a price varying between
$15 and $30.

QUELLI DELLA NOTTE

6834 St. Laurent Blvd.
(St. Lawrence), Mount Royal
(514) 271-3929
Italian restaurant with a sushi
counter. 1930's ambiance.
Homemade pasta. At lunch, the
table d'hôte is available for
between $15 and $30 and during
the evening between $20 and
$40. Private room with a capacity
of 50 people available. Italian
wines. Open sliding doors during
the summer.

RESTO SANS NOM

9700 Blvd. St. Michel,
North End
(514) 389-6732
Italian restaurant specializing in pastas. Limited but very refined menu. Casual ambiance and without pretension.

RESTO VIVALDI

13071 Blvd. Gouin West,
West Island
(514) 620-9200
Small cordial restaurant at an affordable price. Personalized ambiance. A good variety of dishes. Reservation needed on Saturdays. Open during the evening only. Closed on Mondays.

RESTOFIORE

705 St. Catherine St. West
(entrance on McGill College),
Downtown
(514) 288-7777
Typically Italian and French cuisine. Perfect for business people and for sports nights. Relaxed environment. Separate bar and nonsmoking section. Table d'hôte offered during dinner includes an entrée, salad, main dish and mussels.

RIBERA

6001 de Jumonville, East End
(514) 259-3238
Small typical Italian restaurant. Romantic ambiance at night and ideal for business people during lunch hours. Table d'hôte offered during lunch and dinner. Specialties: veal and house pastas.

RISTORANTE FRESCO

6040 Blvd. des Grandes-Prairies, East End
(514) 329-1904
High-quality Italian restaurant. Sophisticated ambiance. Great selection of dishes: grilled meats, seafood, veal and pizzas. Table d'hôte between $15 and $25.

RISTORANTE LINGUINI

18990 rte. Transcanadienne West, West Island
(514) 457-4216
Rustic Italian restaurant with a wooden interior. Cordial and courteous ambiance. Varied menu, fast and experienced service. Table d'hôte offered during lunch and dinner. Delicious entrées.

RISTORANTE SAPORI PRONTO

4894 Sherbrooke St. West.
West End
(514) 487-9666
Fine Italian cuisine, chic, comfortable and plush ambiance. Table d'hôte offered during lunch and dinner. Excellent variety of typical Italian dishes: pastas, grilled meats, risottos and a good choice of desserts.

ROBERTO

2221 Bélanger East, North End

(514) 374-9844

Typical Italian cuisine with a cordial ambiance. Specialties: pastas and homemade ice creams. Menu during the day and table d'hôte at night. Capacity of at least 100 clients with a reception room of 50 places.

ROSELINA

1000 de la Gauchetière West, Downtown

(514) 876-4373

Restaurant with a large covered terrasse that is used year-long. Different menu each day. Specialties: pasta, veal, langoustines (à la carte) and pizzas.

SERENATA (LA)

53 Blvd. Brunswick, West Island

(514) 684-1321

Restaurant of fine cuisine with a rustic and wooden decor. Fireplace used during the winter. Table d'hôte offered during lunch and dinner. Typical Italian restaurant. Excellent wine selection. Courteous and experienced service.

SILA (LA)

2040 St. Denis, Plateau

(514) 844-5083

Fine Italian cuisine. Cordial ambiance. Home-style pasta. Table d'hôte offered during lunch and dinner includes an entrée and coffee.

STROMBOLI

1019 Mount Royal East, Plateau

(514) 528-5020

Restaurant suitable for every palate. Cordial with an excellent home-style cuisine. Lunch table d'hôte includes an entrée, main dish and coffee.

TAORMINA

2530 St. Joseph, West Island

(514) 634-5548

Fine Italian cuisine. Romantic and casual ambiance. Specialties: seafood, homemade pasta and veal. Reception room, two terrasses and free parking.

TARANTELLA (LA)

184 Jean Talon East, Mount Royal

(514) 278-3067

Fine Italian cuisine. Restaurant with a terrasse on the Jean Talon market side and a bistro section. Traditional and modern dishes. Fresh pasta.

TERRACOTTA

1873 St. Louis, North End

(514) 748-6000

Romantic decor. Includes a private room with a capacity of 30 people. Plates prepared with great care. Always fresh ingredients, great quality meat. It is preferable to reserve.
www.restaurantterracotta.com

TIRAMISU ITALIEN

1612 Fleury East, North End
(514) 388-9911
Fine Italian cuisine specializing in fresh fish. The lunch table d'hôte includes coffee, dessert, soup or salad, and the evening table d'hôte includes a choice of six entrées, dessert and coffee. A wide selection of quality wines. Reception room available.

TONY DU SUD

25 Fairmount West, Plateau
(514) 274-7339
Small family restaurant, excellent for family outings and for special occasions. Excellent quality/price value. Home-style cuisine. Menu changes often. Bring your own wine.

TOUR DE PISE CHEZ MAGNANI (LA)

9245 Lajeunesse, North End
(514) 387-5959
Fine, traditional cuisine. Menu includes grilled meats, seafood and pastas. Typical Italian ambiance.

TRATTORIA

1263 Bélanger East, North End
(514) 271-5181
Traditional restaurant. Lunch menu for as little as $8. Good selection of pastas, pizzas, veal and calamari. Reservation for big groups. Discover: the veal and pasta festival which includes soup, main dish, salad, coffee and dessert.

TRATTORIA AUX 3 CONTINENTS

1112 Wolfe, East End
(514) 524-4600
Cavern-style restaurant. Typically Italian with a large variety of dishes: seafood, veal and homemade pasta. Table d'hôte offered during lunch and dinner include an entrée, main dish, coffee and dessert.

TRATTORIA CAPRICCIOSA

5220 Decarie Blvd., Mount Royal
(514) 487-1234
Small restaurant of fine cuisine. Friendly, romantic and typical Italian ambiance. Select wines. Musicians on Fridays and Saturdays. Reception room, terrasse and free parking.

TRATTORIA DAI BAFFONI

6859 St. Laurent Blvd.
(St. Lawrence), Mount Royal
(514) 270-3715
Typical Italian restaurant. Specialties: homemade pasta and veal. Beautiful ambiance, perfect for family outings and romantic dinners. Reception room, free parking. Music on weekends.

TRATTORIA DEL GALLO NERO

5138 Jarry East, East End
(514) 955-9111
Fine Italian cuisine with an antipasto bar. Generous portions. Excellent value for the money. Reservations are preferable.

TRATTORIA DEL TEATRO

1437 Crescent, Downtown
(514) 842-9394
19th century house converted
into an Italian steakhouse. Two
floors and two dining rooms.
Professional service. Fresh meat
and fish.

TRATTORIA I DUE AMICI

2291 Fleury East, North End
(514) 389-0449
Fine cuisine specializing in fresh
pastas and veal. Modern
ambiance. Excellent for outings
between friends. Table d'hôte
offered during lunch and dinner.

TRATTORIA LA VILLETTA

1898 Blvd. Thimens,
North End
(514) 337-1999
Italian home-style cuisine.
Charming establishment. Varied
choices of dishes. Table d'hôte
offered during lunch and dinner.

TRATTORIA TRESTEVERE

1237 Crescent, Downtown
(514) 866-3226
Restaurant of fine Italian cuisine.
Family ambiance. Great selection
of pastas, seafood and veal.

TRE MARIE (LES)

6934 Clark, Mount Royal
(514) 277-9859
Typical Italian restaurant. Home-
style cuisine. The table d'hôte
offered during lunch and dinner is
different every day.

VIA ROMA

7064 St. Laurent Blvd.
(St. Lawrence), Mount Royal
(514) 277-3301
Typical Italian cuisine and
ambiance. Varied menu:
homemade pasta, seafood, fish
and pizza. Table d'hôte is only
served during lunch and includes
an entrée, main dish and coffee.
External terrasse open year long.

VIEILLE CHEMINÉE (à LA)

6715 aut. Métropolitaine East,
East End
(514) 328-7136
Rustic, friendly and intimate
ambiance with a wood oven.
Varied menu: house pastas,
grilled meats, pizzas, veal and
seafood. Reception room with
musicians available on request.
Open on Sundays upon
reservation.

VIEUX FOUR MANAGO (LE)

3636 Blvd. St. Charles,
West Island
(514) 428-0100
Restaurant specializing in pizzas
cooked in a wood oven. Cordial
ambiance around the oven. Table
d'hôte offered during the evening
and special of the day offered
every day. Terrasse with 60
places open during the summer.

VITO (CHEZ)

7655 Decarie Blvd.,
Mount Royal
(514) 735-3623
Restaurant located in the Ruby Foo's Hotel. Each customer is served according to their preference. Prepared game meats and meat offals. Private rooms among the reception rooms of the Ruby Foo's Hotel. Reserve for business or family outings.

WEINSTEN & GAVINOS

1434 Crescent, Downtown
(514) 288-2231
Cuisine specializing in homemade pasta, pizzas, grilled meats and salads. Two floors with a capacity of 400. Cordial ambiance with a modern decor. Happy hour (5 pm to 7 pm) is not to be missed!

Laval & North Shore

BAROLO

2200 Blvd. Labelle, Laval
(450) 682-7450
Large family restaurant. Table d'hôte served every night; lunch specials. Romantic and perfect ambiance for special occasions.

DA TONY MASSARELLI

420 Blvd. des Laurentides,
Laval
(450) 668-3060
Romantic Italian restaurant with a musician and two singers: Tony Massarelli and Jony Valenti. Table d'hôte with a choice between nine principal dishes: pasta, lamb, chicken, veal, fish. Varied menu. Special menu for children. A good place to have a great dinner-dancing night.

EAST SIDE MARIO'S

1775 Blvd. St. Martin West,
Laval
(450) 682-8866
American-Italian cuisine in the style of New York's Little Italy. Family ambiance; New York decor. Menu includes pizzas, pastas, grilled chicken, salads, mussels and hamburgers.

EAST SIDE MARIO'S

401 Blvd. Curé Labelle, Laval
(450) 433-8818

GIORGIO

100 ch. St. François Xavier,
Candiac
(450) 635-7717
Italian restaurant. Excellent cuisine, low prices, great for family outings. Courteous and fast service. Table d'hôte includes soup, main dish, coffee and dessert. Specialties: pastas, pizzas, veal and chicken with sauce.

GIORGIO

257 Blvd. Labelle, Rosemere
(450) 435-5026

GRIGLIATTA (LA)

2225 aut. des Laurentides –
Hotel Hilton Laval
(450) 682-2225
Fine cuisine specializing in grilled
Italian, French and Greek dishes.
Located close to a club. Table
d'hôte offered during lunch;
dinner and brunch on Sundays.
The kitchen is located in the
middle of the dinning room.

GUALDIERI

2016 Blvd. René Laennec,
Laval
(450) 669-9759
Fine authentic Italian cuisine.
Good choices of pastas. Friendly
service. Delivery service
available.

MILANAIS (LE)

2277 Blvd. Le Corbusier, Laval
(450) 973-1118
Small restaurant offering fine
Italian home-style cooking.
Casual and cordial decor.
Specialties: veal scallopine and
fresh pasta. Excellent value for
the price.

NEGRONI (LE)

192 Blvd. St. Rose, Laval
(450) 687-6912
Cordial restaurant, open for over
23 years. Italian decor. Table
d'hôte offered during lunch and
dinner includes an entrée, main
dish and a dessert. Perfect for
business people.

PALMO

533 Principale, Laval
(450) 689-4141
A pleasant restaurant, ideal for
romantic dinners or family
evenings. Establishment with a
fireplace and a terrasse. Large
variety of dishes: seafood, veal,
game meats, grilled meats.
Reception room for big groups.

PICCOLO MONDO

1150 Blvd. Curé Labelle, Laval
(450) 681-1609
Fine cuisine specializing in
homemade pastas, seafood and
veal. Excellent selection of
imported wines. Cordial and
typical Italian ambiance. Capacity
of 120 clients with a reception
room.

PIRATE DE LAVAL (LE)

802 Blvd. des Laurentides,
Laval
(450) 668-0780
Restaurant decorated like an old
boat, specializing in seafood.
Musician trio on Fridays. Table
d'hôte offered during lunch and
dinner.

RISTORANTE LUGANO'S

1723 Blvd. St. Martin West,
Laval
(450) 686-1888
Typical Italian restaurant,
moderately priced. Cordial and
romantic ambiance. Very good
selection of dishes. Table d'hôte
offered during lunch and dinner.

Come and be pleasantly surprised.

SAVERIO

1365 Blvd. Curé Labelle, Laval
(450) 686-8669
Restaurant with dinner-dancing on Wednesday through Sunday. Menu and table d'hôte with 11 choices in the evening. Buffets for business lunches. Capacity of 200 clients with a conference room.

TERRACINA

2070 Blvd. Curé Labelle, Laval
(450) 973-4143
Fine traditional Italian cuisine. Excellent quality/price value. Friendly and courteous service.

TOTO'S

1670 St. Martin West, Laval
(450) 680-1499
Restaurant of fine Italian cuisine. Table d'hôte offered during lunch and dinner includes a soup or a salad and coffee or tea. Perfect for family outings.

VIEUX FOUR (AU)

300 Sicard, Laval
(450) 437-4100
Magnificent restaurant that has a stone floor and a wooden roof. Pizza cooked in a wood oven. Good pasta, steak, veal and chicken. Café that offers an amazing happy hour (5 pm to 7 pm), Monday through Friday. Large terrasse during the summer.

VIEUX FOUR DE LAVAL (LE)

5070 Blvd. Lévesque East, Laval
(450) 661-7711
The original 'Vieux Four' restaurant. Excellent quality/price value. Rustic decor. Table d'hôte starting at $16 during dinner and $11 during lunch. Pizzas are cooked in a wood oven, pasta al dente, great selection of renowned wines. Always fresh ingredients.

SOUTH SHORE

CASA MICHELANGELO

4815 Taschereau Blvd., Greenfield Park
(450) 445-0991
Restaurant of fine cuisine. Table d'hôte offered during lunch and dinner. Five entrées during the evening and three during the day. Varied menu: fish, seafood, ribs, pastas, etc.

CHUTES DU RICHELIEU (AUX)

486 1re Rue, Richelieu
(450) 658-6689
Italian restaurant with windows on three sides with a view of the river. Table d'hôte starts at $19. Brunches on Sunday from 11 am to 2:30 pm.

DANVITO
154 Blvd. Sir Wilfrid Laurier,
Beloeil
(450) 464-5166
Small romantic restaurant.
Specialties: seafood, meats and
pastas. Table d'hôte every
evening.

EAST SIDE MARIO'S
1166 Volta, Boucherville
(450) 641-3993
American-Italian cuisine in the
style of New York's Little Italy.
Family ambiance; New York
decor. Menu includes pizzas,
pastas, grilled chicken, salads,
mussels and hamburgers.

EAST SIDE MARIO'S
7350 Taschereau Blvd.,
Brossard
(450) 671-2223

FRANCO ET NINO
590 Blvd. St. Charles,
Vaudreuil
(450) 455-9300
Traditional and cordial ambiance.
Home-style cuisine. Table d'hôte
includes a choice of six entrées,
12 main dishes, coffee and
dessert. Varied menu: soups, veal
escalope, seafood, chicken,
rabbit, 100 kinds of wines. Two
dining rooms, perfect for
business people. Also offers wine
classes.

GIORGIO
3626 Taschereau Blvd.,
Greenfield Park
(450) 465-2002

GIORGIO
95 Blvd. de Mortagne,
Boucherville
(450) 655-8422

ITALIA
192 Blvd. Curé-Poirier West,
Longueuil
(450) 679-3640
Restaurant which serves take-out
dishes only. Great selection of
dishes, including pizzas.
Everything is homemade; fast
service.

LUIGGI
3271 Taschereau Blvd. East,
Greenfield Park
(450) 671-1617
Restaurant with two sections.
Specialties: pastas, filet mignon,
seafood. A different table d'hôte
every day. Cordial and casual
ambiance. Breakfast served every
day (served on a terrasse during
weekends).

MEZZALUNA RISTORANTE ITALIANO
68 St. Charles,
St. Jean sur Richelieu
(450) 358-9333
Small restaurant of fine authentic
Italian cuisine specializing in
homemade pastas, veal and
seafood. Try their calamari, an
undeniable delight.

NOVELLO

680A de Montbrun,
Boucherville
(450) 449-7227
Italian restaurant, romantic
ambiance. Variety of meats, pasta
and seafood. Table d'hôte offered
during lunch and dinner includes
an entrée, main dish, coffee and
dessert.

OLIVETO (L')

205 St. Jean, Longueuil
(450) 677-8743
Fine Mediterranean cuisine.
Modern ambiance. Large wine
cellar with an excellent selection
of the Italian wines. Table d'hôte
offered during lunch and dinner.

PIAZZA ITALIA

1791 Principale, St. Julie
(450) 649-8080
Specializing in fine Italian cuisine.
Good choice of homemade pasta
and seafood. Charming ambiance.
Capacity of 120 clients.

PINOCCHIO

151 St. Charles West,
Longueuil
(450) 442-2111
Restaurant of fine Italian cuisine.
Cordial ambiance. Private room.
Table d'hôte offered during lunch
and dinner. Fresh fish offered
every day.

RESTO LE FOUR DE BELOEIL

20 Blvd. St. Jean Baptiste,
Beloeuil
(450) 536-3687
Casual restaurant. Specialties:
pastas and pizzas. Tuesdays, two
for one; Wednesdays, all you can
eat mussels. Breakfast served on
Saturdays and Sundays. Table
d'hôte offered during lunch and
dinner. Small bar available for
those waiting and a private
lounge on the second floor.

RISTORANTE LA BARCA

540 rte. Marie-Victorin,
Boucherville
(450) 641-2277
Fine typical Italian cuisine.
Specialties: seafood, pastas and
pizzas cooked in a wood oven.
Homemade pastas and desserts.
Cordial, romantic and family
ambiance. Reception room with a
capacity from 20 to 80 people.
Terrasse and pergola during the
summer.

ROMA ANTIQUA (LA)

4900 Taschereau Blvd.,
Greenfield Park
(450) 672-2211
Good quality/price value. Family
ambiance. Good selection of
dishes. Bring your own wine.
Excellent entrées, like the fried
calamari. Try the pasta trio.

SICILIEN (LE)
514 du Séminaire N.,
St. Jean sur Richelieu
(450) 348-6600
Charming, intimate ambiance.
Table d'hôte offered during lunch
and dinner. Good variety of
pastas, pizzas and steaks.
Capacity of 50 clients; delivery
service available.

TAVOLA (LA)
352 Guillaume, Longueuil
(450) 928-1433
Small local restaurant with a
cordial ambiance. Splendid
European-style terrasse.
Specialties: homemade smoked
salmon and fresh pastas.

TRATTORIA LA TERRAZZA
575 Victoria, St. Lambert
(450) 672-7422
Classic Italian restaurant. Typical
home-style cuisine. Specialties:
homemade pasta, seafood and
veal. Capacity of 80 clients and
70 on the terrasse. Establishment
located in the downtown area.

TRE COLORI
1696 Bourgogne, Chambly
(450) 658-6653
Tasty Italian home-style cuisine.
One of the best pizzas on the
south-shore; homemade pasta.
Table d'hôte offered during
dinner includes main dishes and
coffee. Excellent quality/price
value.

VILLA BELLA (LA)
2070 Victoria,
Greenfield Park
(450) 672-4727
Affordable Italian cuisine. Plush,
intimate and romantic ambiance.
Try as an entrée: brie with pesto
on garlic bread.

VILLA MASSIMO
120 Taschereau Blvd.,
La Prairie
(450) 444-3416
Four star restaurant. Fine
exquisite cuisine. All is
homemade: pastas, breads,
desserts, etc. 20,000 wine
bottles. Three separate rooms
and a fourth royal room for big
receptions. Open for over 28
years. Music on Fridays and
Saturdays. It is preferable to
reserve during the weekend.

VINO BIANCO
564 Blvd. Adolphe-Chapleau
(450) 965-8814
Fine Italian cuisine specializing in
homemade pasta and pizzas
cooked in a wood oven. Cordial
ambiance. Affordable business
lunches and table d'hôte.

◎ *Japanese*

ISLAND OF MONTREAL

ATAMI
5499 Côte des Neiges,
Mount Royal
(514) 735-5400
Small cordial restaurant with a
sushi counter. Large terrasse with

a capacity from 30 to 40 people during the summer. Table d'hôte offered during lunch and dinner includes an entrée, salad, main dish, dessert and tea. $5 fee for any delivery.

AZUMA

5263 St. Laurent Blvd. (St. Lawrence), Plateau
(514) 271-5263
Traditional Japanese cuisine. Specialties: sushi and tempuras. Traditional ambiance, tatami rooms and a sushi counter. Capacity of 40 clients.

BENI HANA GRILL

5666 Sherbrooke St. East, East End
(514) 256-1694
Specialties: sushi, sashimis, aloyaux, filet mignon and shrimp. Complete dinner for as low as $16. Rectangular tables where the chef cooks directly in front of you. Very entertaining.

BENI HANA GRILL

7965 Decarie Blvd., Mount Royal
(514) 731-8205

BLEU CARAMEL

4517 de La Roche, Plateau
(514) 526-0005
Good Japanese soup and noodle selection. Dinner is served in tatami rooms. Elegant decor. Enjoyable selection of sushi.

GEISHA SUSHI

1597 St. Hubert, Plateau
(514) 524-8484
Fine Japanese cuisine. Authentic meals for the aficionados among us. Table d'hôte offered during lunch and dinner includes the main dish, bento box, soup, salad, dessert and Japanese tea. Personalized service.

HYANG JIN

5332 Queen Mary, Mount Royal
(514) 482-0645
Fine Japanese cuisine. Excellent ambiance with Asian music. Table d'hôte offered during lunch and dinner includes an entrée, soup, main dish and salad. Varied menu.

ISAKAYA

3469 Park Ave., Plateau
(514) 845-8226
Authentic cuisine. Specialties: grilled sushi and fish. Modern ambiance with a little bistro. Table d'hôte includes salad, soup and main dish. Prices during lunch start at $7. Prices during dinner are a little more expensive.

KASHIMA

1232 Greene, West End
(514) 934-0962
Authentic Japanese cuisine; Asian music. Perfect ambiance for business people during lunch hours and for intimate dinners in the evenings. Free Japanese tea.

Always fresh ingredients and plates are prepared with great care.

KOBE STEAKHOUSE
6720 Sherbrooke St. East,
East End
(514) 254-9926
Japanese restaurant where the chefs give you a show. Varied menu, 2-for-1 and a table d'hôte that includes salad, main dish, vegetables, rice, noodles and dessert. Refreshing experience.

MAÏKO SUSHI
387 Bernard West,
Mount Royal
(514) 490-1225
Japanese restaurant with a family ambiance. Modern, recently renovated. Private lounge. Table d'hôte offered during lunch and dinner includes two entrées, main dish, dessert and tea.

MIKASA SUSHI BAR
2049 Peel, Downtown
(514) 907-8282
Fine Japanese cuisine. Cordial ambiance, modern music and prestigious decor. Sushi counter, open kitchen, table d'hôte, business dinner and menu à la carte.

MIKASA SUSHI BAR
9835 Blvd. de l'Acadie,
North End
(514) 336-8282

MIYAKO
1439 Amherst, East End
(514) 521-5329
Restaurant without pretension with a sushi counter and tatami rooms. Menu is composed of different sushi and sashimis prepared with a variety of seafood and fish. Popular eating place.

NAGANO SUSHI
7655 Decarie Blvd.,
Mount Royal
(514) 735-4452
Restaurant located in the Ruby Foo Hotel. Great selection of typical Japanese dishes. Refined cuisine, sushi and sashimis. Modern and elegant ambiance.

NAGOYA
140 Notre Dame West,
Old Montreal
(514) 845-5864
Restaurant with sushi and Korean barbecue. Relaxed, elegant and authentic Japanese ambiance. Six choices of tables d'hôtes include an entrée, large salad, main dish and tea.

OSAKA
2137 de Bleury, Downtown
(514) 849-3438
Japanese restaurant, family ambiance, affordable prices. Try the soups with ramen noodles and soba.

SAKATA

3977 St. Laurent Blvd. (St. Lawrence), Plateau
(514) 284-3828
Specialties: teriyaki, salmon, tempuras and sushi. Great selection offered à la carte. Table d'hôte includes miso soup, tempura entrées, teriyaki or sushi as a main dish, roasted ice cream, coffee or tea. A choice of a hundred makis and sushi. Two tatami rooms.

SAKURA GARDEN

2114 Mountain (de la Montagne), Downtown
(514) 288-9122
Relaxed and elegant Japanese restaurant with a sushi bar. Lunch special includes soup, main dish and dessert. Menu à la carte. Open for over 25 years.

SHO-DAN*

2020 Metcalfe, Downtown
(514) 987-9987
Restaurant with a sushi bar and a modern ambiance. Personalized menu à la carte and table d'hôte. Two tatami rooms, capacity of 20 people. Try the 'flower' tuna and the Romeo and Juliette rolls.

SHO-DAN*

1425 René Levesque (fka Dorchester), Downtown
(514) 871-0777
*Featured establishment
see p. 188

SUSHI OGURA

2025 Union, Downtown
(514) 847-9000
Small restaurant. Specialties: sushi, tempuras and teriyaki dishes. Authentic cuisine with a sushi counter. Traditional ambiance.

TAKARA

1455 Peel, Downtown
(514) 849-9796
Traditional Japanese restaurant: shoji folding screens, sushi counters and tatami rooms. Lunch special. Large variety of dishes, including a combo for two.

TOKYO SUKIYAKI

7355 Mountain Sights, Mount Royal
(514) 737-7245
Traditional restaurant with tatami rooms and shoji folding screens. Very serene ambiance. Specialties: sushi, tempuras, teriyaki and chicken yakitori. Bento boxes for children. Several specials and combos offered in the evening. Closed for lunch.

TOKYO SUSHI BAR

4805 Sources Blvd., West Island
(514) 685-7082
Fine authentic cuisine with a sushi counter. Table d'hôte available. Three tatami rooms with shoji folding screens. Capacity of 90 clients.

TOYO GRILLADE

2155 Mountain (de la
Montagne), Downtown
(514) 844-9292
Menu composed of various sushi
and other Japanese preparations.
Their filet mignon are not to be
missed. Gracious service.

WAKAMONO

1251 Mount Royal East,
Plateau
(514) 527-2747
Japanese cuisine. Specialties:
sushi, fresh fish and noodles
(ramen, soba, harusame and
udon). Friendly and popular
ambiance.

WISUSHI

3697 St. John's Blvd.,
West Island
(514) 696-3399
Cordial and modern place with a
sushi counter. Relaxed ambiance
with jazz music. Lunch specials
from Monday to Friday. Table
d'hôte offered during the evening
includes a soup, salad and ten
choices suggested by the chef.
Dinner for two specials also
available. Good wine selection.
Nonsmoking restaurant.

YAKATA

5412 Côte des Neiges,
Mount Royal
(514) 733-9101
Japanese restaurant with a sushi
counter. Good quality/price value.
Table d'hôte includes salad, soup,
a sushi entrée and the main dish.

LAVAL & NORTH SHORE

DÉLICES DE TOKYO

1224 Blvd. Curé Labelle, Laval
(450) 688-8010
Authentic cuisine. Specialty:
sushi. Japanese music and decor.
Table d'hôte includes a salad,
entrée, soup, main dish, dessert,
coffee or tea. Two private rooms.

ONYX SUSHI ET GRILLADES

1545 Blvd. Corbusier, Laval
(450) 978-5075
Grand Japanese restaurant.
Specialties: grilled meats and
sushi. Modern ambiance, perfect
for business people. Special: 40%
off sushi on Wednesdays. Great
selection in the à la carte menu.
Bar Foxy on the second floor.

TOYO GRILLADES à LA JAPONAISE

1510 Chomedey, Laval
(450) 688-4020
Menu composed of various sushi
and other Japanese delights.
Dishes are prepared in front of
the customers. Gracious service.
South Shore

WISUSHI

2161 Blvd. des Laurentides
(450) 669-3862
Cordial and modern place with a
sushi counter. Relaxed ambiance
with jazz music. Lunch specials
from Monday to Friday. Table
d'hôte offered during the evening
includes a soup, salad and 10
choices suggested by the chef.
Dinner for two specials also

available. Good wine selection. Nonsmoking restaurant.

SOUTH SHORE

SHOGUN (1983)
6155 Taschereau Blvd., Brossard
(450) 678-3868
Restaurant of fine Japanese cuisine with a sushi counter and heated tables. Semi-modern ambiance. Table d'hôte offered every day. Tatami room and summer terrasse.

◎ *Jewish*

ERNIE & ELLIE'S PLACE
6900 Decarie Blvd., Mount Royal
(514) 344-4444
Kosher restaurant with two kitchens: Asian (sushi, Chinese) and Canadian (grilled meats, steaks, hamburgers). Table d'hôte and special offered every day. Delivery service available with orders of $10 or more. Free parking: underground and exterior.

◎ *Korean*

HWANG-KUM
5908 Sherbrooke St. West, West End
(514) 487-1712
Cuisine with a good variety of soups. Specialty: sweetened marinated beef bulgogi. Menu includes combos for two. Excellent pork and BBQ beef.

Korean decor. Take-out service available.

QUATRE SAISONS
4200 St. Jacques, South End
(514) 932-3309
Authentic Korean cuisine with a selection of Japanese dishes. Good quality/price value. Every day specials.

SUL AC JUNG
3300 Cavendish, West End
(514) 489-6656
Korean restaurant specializing in table barbecues. Fine cuisine. Authentic and casual ambiance. Private room for groups. Take-out service available.

◎ *Latin American*

BAYOU-BRASIL
4552 St. Denis, Plateau
(514) 847-0088
Brazilian, Cajun and Creole cuisine. Brazilian environment with colonial decorations and ambiance music: bossa nova, samba and jazz.

CHERO
5761 Jean Talon East, East End
(514) 255-2000
Peruvian restaurant located in a St. Leonard shopping center. Typical dishes from the pacific coast. Choice of different grilled meats, fish and seafood. Specialties include jalea mariscos, grouper ceviche and black conch. Cordial ambiance.

COIN DU MEXIQUE (LE)

2489 Jean Talon East,
North End
(514) 374-7448
Mexican cuisine. Popular dishes:
tacos, grilled meat, enchiladas
and other feasts. Sharply
coloured decor. Cordial Latin
ambiance.

ECHE PA' ECHARLA

7216 St. Hubert, North End
(514) 276-3243
Authentic Peruvian cuisine.
Specialty: maritime dishes. Calm
service and simple decor.
Unpretentious menu.

EL CHALAN

520 Beaubien East, North End
(514) 272-5585
Peruvian restaurant serving a
great selection of entrées,
seafood and meats. Try the soup-
meals. Ethnic ambiance with
Spanish television.

EL JIBARO

7183 St. Hubert, North End
(514) 948-4827
Restaurant serving authentic
Peruvian cuisine in a traditional
decor. House specialty: lovers'
soup. Good choice of seafood,
brochettes and other Peruvian
specialties.

EL TACO DEL TABARNACO

916 Duluth East, Plateau
(514) 528-9865
Latin restaurant whose pleasant
decor includes palm trees.

Affordable meals and quick
service specializing in fajitas and
juice.

IRAZU

1028 St. Zotique East,
North End
(514) 279-0027
Fine Costa Rican cuisine: grilled
meats, seafood, fish and
traditional soups. Try their carne
casado. The noon and evening
table d'hôte includes an entrée,
the main dish and a dessert.
Traditional decor.

LAS PALMAS PUPUSERIA

632 Jarry East, North End
(514) 270-7334
Salvadorian restaurant. Bring
your own wine. Specialties:
pupusas, tacos, burritos and
grilled meats. Simple selection
offering generous portions.

LÉLÉ DE CUCA

70 Marie Anne East, Plateau
(514) 849-6649
Small intimate restaurant that
serves generous portions of
chicken and seafood. Bring your
own wine. Capacity of 40.
Nonsmoking establishment. Open
for over 22 years.

MELCHORITA

7901 St. Dominique,
North End
(514) 382-2129
Homemade Peruvian cuisine.
Specialties include ceviches and
fried squid, among others.

Breakfasts available every day. Excellent value for money.

MILSA (LE)

1445 Bishop, Downtown
(514) 985-0777
Brazilian steakhouse: churrascaria. Brazilian dancers from 8 pm to 9 pm every evening. Open 7 days a week. Specialty: grilled meats on wooden charcoal.

SENZALA

177 Bernard West, Plateau
(514) 274-1464
Restaurant with live music. Bar offers Brazilian tropical cocktails. To be tried: the ceviche, the mariscada and the garlic marinated octopus. Brunch on Sundays.

ⓖ *Lebanese/Syrian*

Island of Montreal

ALEP

199 Jean Talon East, Mount Royal
(514) 270-6396
Restaurant of fine cuisine, bistro and terrasse. Typical Syrian ambiance. Menu à la carte only.

ALKANATER

220 Blvd. Crémazie West, North End
(514) 858-6999
Fine Lebanese cuisine with a traditional ambiance. Belly dancers and Lebanese singers

from Friday to Sunday. Reception room available for groups.

BERMA

222 Blvd. Crémazie East, North End
(514) 389-7117
Lebanese and Syrian cuisine. Try: the shish taouk and the shawarma. Capacity of 50 clients. Open seven days a week. Authentic Lebanese decor. Family ambiance.

DAOU

2373 Blvd. Marcel Laurin, North End
(514) 334-1199
Pleasant restaurant of Lebanese home-style cooking. Authentic dishes and decor. Friendly and courteous ambiance. Varied menu: chicken, grilled meats, raw meat. Extremely succulent hummus. Their catering service is exceptional.

DAOU

519 Faillon East, North End
(514) 276-8310

DIMA

1575 Dudemaine, North End
(514) 334-3876
Lebanese cuisine with a touch of Syrian. Dishes are prepared with fresh ingredients. Menu includes hummus, metabal, muhammara, grilled meats and Armenian sausages. Everything is homemade.

LILAS (AUX)

5570 Park Ave., Plateau
(514) 271-1453
Tasty and excellent cuisine for
groups who like to share.
Possibility of making
combinations of small dishes.
Cuisine without pretension and
rich in flavour. Family ambiance.

SAMIRAMISS

885 Decarie Blvd., North End
(514) 747-3085
Lebanese home-style cooking.
Family ambiance and cordial
environment. Summer terrasse.
Specialties: grilled Lebanese
meats and seafood. Specials and
menu à la carte are offered every
day.

SIRÈNE DE LA MER (LA)

114 Dresden, Mount Royal
(514) 345-0345
Charming restaurant of fine
Lebanese cuisine. Chic ambiance;
elegant and yet family oriented.
Specialties: roasted fish and
seafood. Possibility of choosing
your own fish, always fresh.

SIRÈNE DE LA MER (LA)

1805 l'Acadie, North End
(514) 332-2255

TENTE (LA)

1125 Decarie Blvd., North End
(514) 747-7876
Lebanese and Mediterranean
restaurant with two services:
take-out counter and restaurant
of fine cuisine. Specialty:

Lebanese brochettes. Narghiles
are available.

ZAWEDEH

3407 Peel, Downtown
(514) 288-4141
Located in the Best Western
hotel,this establishment has a bar
and lounge. Table d'hôte offered
during lunch and dinner. Chic and
modern ambiance. Specialties:
Lebanese and Mediterranean
cuisine. Orchestra and belly
dancers on Fridays and
Saturdays.

LAVAL & NORTH SHORE

AL SULTAN

145 Blvd. Curé Labelle, Laval
(450) 688-4723
Fine Lebanese cuisine. Arab
ambiance. Varied menu à la carte
and specials going from $25 to
$50 including entrée, main dish,
cafta, fruits and coffee.

LORDIA

3883 Blvd. Perron, Laval
(450) 681-4438
Fine Lebanese cuisine. Traditional
ambiance, narghiles and shows
on weekends. Specialty: cooking
on wooden charcoal. Reception
room available.

MÈRE MILIA (LA)

3005 Blvd. Cartier West,
Laval
(450) 688-0404
Large reception room, capacity of
250 clients, fine Lebanese

cuisine. Belly dancers and orchestra on request.

◎ *Mediterranean*

BISTRO PHILINOS
4806 Park Ave., Plateau
(514) 271-9099
Mediterranean restaurant with a varied menu. Ancient Byzantine decor. Special of the day offered every day starting at $8. Musicians are available upon request.

GUSTO
1380 Notre Dame West, Downtown
(514) 939-2130
Fine Italian and Peruvian cuisine. Good ambiance. Excellent authentic cuisine. Good quality/price value.

JOYA
6918 St. Laurent Blvd. (St. Lawrence), Mount Royal
(514) 271-3840
Mediterranean cuisine. Specialties: homemade pastas, fresh fish and great quality meats. Varied menu. Special of the week changes every week. Popular establishment. Music on weekends.

MEDI MEDI
479 St. Alexis, Old Montreal
(514) 284-2195
Mediterranean bar open during lunch hours only. Mediterranean

decor, ceramics and two slates. The lunch express special includes steak, fries and beer. Table d'hôte includes a soup, salad and a main dish.

MEZZÉ
3449 St. Laurent Blvd. (St. Lawrence), Plateau
(514) 281-0275
Greek bistro. Specialty: fresh fish. Try: seafood brochettes, swordfish and other fried fish.

PIZZELLA (LA)
2080 St. Mathieu, Downtown
(514) 939-3030
Restaurant specializing in fine Mediterranean cuisine. Romantic ambiance. Excellent value.

RHODOS BAY
5583 Park Ave., Plateau
(514) 270-1304
Greek islands cuisine. Mediterranean ambiance. Great choice of fresh fish and seafood. Table d'hôte offered during lunch and dinner.

TI AMO
73 Prince Arthur East, Plateau
(514) 843-6660
Mediterranean home-style cooking. Restaurant-bar bistro. Table d'hôte offered during dinner includes a soup, salad and principal dish. Varied menu. Music available on request.

TOUCHEH

351 Prince Albert, West End
(514) 369-6868
Specialties: Mediterranean and
Iranian cuisine. Exotic ambiance
and decor. Varied menu, including
several Mediterranean, Iranian
and European dishes. Always
fresh ingredients. Bring your own
wine.

LAVAL & NORTH SHORE

CALVI'S

1707 St. Martin West
(450) 680-1656
Fine Mediterranean cuisine.
Specialties: seafood, fresh fish
and grilled meats. Rustic decor.
Table d'hôte offered during lunch
and dinner. Closed on Sundays.
Music on Fridays and Saturdays.

GIOTTO

2440 aut. des Laurentides,
Laval
(450) 687-2440
Mediterranean cuisine centered
mostly on Italian cuisine. Large
variety of dishes, buffet and
brunches. Impeccable service and
a sophisticated ambiance.
Located in the Sheraton.

© *Mexican*

3 AMIGOS

1657 St. Catherine St. West,
Downtown
(514) 939-3329
Very diversified menu: pastas,
fajitas, tacos, hamburgers, chili
and enchiladas. Excellent

quality/price value. Generous
portions. Excellent ambiance for
business dinners and for outings
between friends.

CACTUS

4461 St. Denis, Plateau
(514) 849-0349
Traditional ambiance, Latin music.
Great selection of wine.

CASA DE MATTEO

440 St. François Xavier,
Old Montreal
(514) 844-7448
Traditional ambiance and music.
Excellent menu à la carte and
lunch specials. Music on Fridays
and Saturdays.

EL MESON

1678 Blvd. St. Joseph,
West Island
(514) 634-0442
Traditional Mexican home-style
cooking. Authentic ambiance, two
terrasses. Table d'hôte offered
during lunch from 11 am to 3 pm.
Menu à la carte also offered.

GUADALUPE (LA)

2345 Ontario East, East End
(514) 523-3262
Authentic Mexican cuisine. Family
ambiance. Generous portions and
good quality.

HACIENDA (LA)

1148 Van Horne, Mount Royal
(514) 270-3043
Small restaurant, beautiful
ambiance. Menu composed of

several popular Mexican dishes. Try their margaritas.

MAÑANA

3605 St. Denis, Plateau
(514) 847-1050
Fine Mexican cuisine. Traditional ambiance. Specialties: fajitas with shrimp, fajitas and vegetarian enchiladas. Table d'hôte offered during dinner and on weekends.

MEXICALI ROSA'S

1425 Bishop, Downtown
(514) 284-0344
Mexican cuisine with a touch of California. Casual ambiance. Menu à la carte only. Specialty: margaritas.

◎ *Morrocan*

CHEZ BADI

1675 de Maisonneuve West, Downtown
(514) 932-6144
Moroccan cuisine. Mediterranean dishes include merguez sandwiches and marinated or roasted veal liver. Narguiles are available.

COUSCOUS ROYAL

919 Duluth East, Plateau
(514) 528-1307
Traditional Moroccan cuisine. Specialties: couscous and barbecue lamb. Table d'hôte includes an entrée, main dish and mint tea. Bring your own wine.

EL MOROCCO

3450 Drummond, Downtown
(514) 844-6888
Moroccan restaurant serving kosher dishes. Ideal ambiance for family outings or for parties. Excellent choices of couscous, tajines and salads.

MENARA (LA)

256 St. Paul East,
Old Montreal
(514) 861-1989
Traditional Moroccan menu. Sublime decor, similar to the 'Thousand and One Nights' stories. Evenings and menu are personalized with the night's theme. Baladi show, perfect for marriages and receptions.

SOLEIL DE MARRAKECH

5131 Decarie Blvd.,
Mount Royal
(514) 485-5238
Fine Moroccan cuisine. Menu includes couscous and different traditional plates. Moroccan ambiance, Arab music. Baladi dancers on weekends and with reservation.

◎ *Pakistani*

SHAHI PALACE

4773 Sources Blvd.,
West Island
(514) 685-0000
Small, authentic Pakistani restaurant serving fine cuisine. Plates are prepared with great care and passion. Their butter

chicken is worth the detour. A must!

◎ *Persian*

BYBLOS LE PETIT CAFÉ

1499 Laurier East, Plateau
(514) 523-9396
Iranian cuisine. Friendly
atmosphere. Lunch express menu
includes a dish and a dessert.
Open sliding doors during the
summer.

◎ *Pizzeria*

PIZZAFIORE

3518 Lacombe, Mount Royal
(514) 735-1555
Cordial ambiance, visible wood
oven and rustic decor. Several
specials. Capacity of 70 clients
with a reception room. Three
terrasses.

PIZZAIOLLE (LA)

4801 St. Denis, Plateau
(514) 499-9711
First authentic pizzeria to use
wood ovens. Great selection of
pizzas and pastas. Modern and
friendly ambiance. The lunch
special includes salad, choice
between three pizzas or pastas,
coffee and dessert

◎ *Polish*

STASH CAFÉ*
200 St. Paul West,
Old Montreal
(514) 845-6611
Traditional Polish restaurant.
Great selection of dishes à la
carte. The dinner table d'hôte
includes a soup, salad, main
dish, dessert and coffee.
**Featured establishment see
p. 190*

◎ *Portuguese*

CASA MINHOTA

3959 St. Laurent Blvd.
(St. Lawrence), Plateau
(514) 842-2661
Specialties: fresh fish, seafood
and rack of lamb. Table d'hôte
offered during lunch and dinner
includes an entrée, main dish,
dessert and coffee.

ROI DU PLATEAU (LE)

51 Rachel West, Plateau
(514) 844-8393
Excellent quality for the price.
Family ambiance. Menu à la carte
only. Music on certain nights.

SOLMAR

111 St. Paul East,
Old Montreal
(514) 861-4562
Specialties: seafood and grilled
meats. Menu includes a three-
dish special starting at $40. This
includes an entrée, soup, salad,
main dish, dessert and coffee.
Terrasse on the first floor.

TASCA
172 Duluth East, Plateau
(514) 987-1530
Fine Portuguese cuisine. Great
selection of dishes: seafood,
fresh fish, steaks and grilled
meats. Table d'hôte offered
during lunch and dinner includes
an entrée, salad, main dish and
dessert. Music on Fridays and
Saturdays.

VINTAGE (LE)
4475 St. Denis, Plateau
(514) 849-4264
Specialty: seafood. Excellent
quality/price value. Intimate and
cordial ambiance. Menu à la carte
has various good selections.

ÉTOILE DE L'OCÉAN (L')
101 Rachel East, Plateau
(514) 844-4588
Traditional cuisine. Good
Portuguese wine selection. Table
d'hôte includes an entrée, main
dish, dessert and coffee. Two
reception rooms with a capacity
of 80 people each.

◎ *Québécois*

SOUTH SHORE

AUBERGE HANDFIELD
555 Richelieu, St. Hilaire
(450) 584-2226
Quebec-style restaurant
specializing in country-style
cooking. Rustic ambiance. Good
game selection and other regional
meats. Table d'hôte offered

during lunch and dinner.
Reception rooms available.

◎ *Resto-Bar*

AVENTURE
438 Pl. Jacques Cartier,
Old Montreal
(514) 866-9439
French and Italian cuisine.
European and modern style
decor. Two floors, capacity of 280
clients and two terrasses.

BACCI ST-DENIS
4205 St. Denis, Plateau
(514) 844-3929
Recently renovated, very chic
appearance. Zen decor. 22 billiard
tables. Vast choice of alcohol.
VIP lounge for groups of 15 to
100 people.

CAFÉ EL DORADO
921 Mount Royal East, Plateau
(514) 598-8282
Restaurant that offers a casual
atmosphere. Breakfast is served
from 7 am to 4 pm during the
week and brunches are served
from 8 am to 3 pm during the
weekends. Varied table d'hôte.
The coffee is grinded on location.
Homemade cheesecakes.

CAFÉ LAÏKA
4040 St. Laurent Blvd.
(St. Lawrence), Plateau
(514) 842-8088
Establishment with a
contemporary design. Large
window facing the street. Varied
menu; coffee/croissants in the

morning; brunches on weekends.
DJ each night.

ENTRACTE (L')

1740 Blvd. René Lévesque
(fka Dorchester) West,
Downtown
(514) 931-8841
Specialties: Italian dishes, in
particular the gnocchis, the
pastas and the filet mignon.
Restaurant with a capacity of
200. Giant screen TV at the bar.

MCLEAN'S PUB

1210 Peel, Downtown
(514) 393-3132
Traditional Irish bar. Varied menu.
Specialty: hamburgers. Winner of
a online poll for the best
hamburgers in town. Eighteen
kinds of beers; variety of
imported beers.

MONKLAND TAVERN

5555 Monkland, West End
(514) 486-5768
Restaurant-bar, animated
ambiance, tavern decor. Varied
menu. Large variety of alcohol.

NYKS

1250 de Bleury, Downtown
(514) 866-1787
Cordial ambiance, pub-style,
friendly service. Wood and brick
decor. Specialties: grilled sirloin
steak and fried calamari.

OLDE ORCHARD PUB & GRILL

5563 Monkland, West End
(514) 484-1569
The Olde Orchard is a
neighbourhood pub. We'd like to
say 'typical', but they are not
common! Great pub atmosphere,
excellent pub food and good
selection of beers. Live Celtic
music on some nights. The crow
is a mix of ages and walks of life.
Large room at the back. Terrasse
in front.

PETITE ARDOISE (LA)

222 Laurier West, Plateau
(514) 495-4961
French cuisine that offers a table
d'hôte during lunch and dinner.
Parisian ambiance and decor with
garden.

PETITE MARCHE (LA)

5037 St. Denis, Plateau
(514) 842-1994
French-Italian cuisine. Renowned
for the energy and kindness of
the service. Art exposition of
local artists. Brunches on
Saturdays and Sundays.

⊚ Rotisserie

BAR-B-BARN

1201 Guy, Downtown
(514) 931-3811
In business for more than 35
years. Chicken and world-
renowned spare ribs. Family
atmosphere.

BAR-B-BARN
3300 Sources Blvd., West Island
(514) 683-0225

BIDDLE'S JAZZ & RIBS
2060 Aylmer, Downtown
(514) 842-8656
Open for over 25 years. Very cordial ambiance. Timbered decor with tiffany lamps. Jazz group every evening.

RÔTISSERIE LAURIER
381 Laurier West, Downtown
(514) 273-3671
Rotisserie established in 1936. Specialty: BBQ chicken. All homemade. Rustic decor.

⊚ Russian

ERMITAGE
5001 Queen Mary, Mount Royal
(514) 735-3886
Restaurant of fine European cuisine. Specialty: Russian gastronomy. Excellent quality/price value. Table d'hôte starting at $9 during lunch.

KALINKA
1409 St. Marc, Downtown
(514) 932-3403
Authentic Russian cuisine. Music during the weekends. Try their Stroganov beef, the steak, the salmon and the filet mignon. Light lunch menu. Simple and attractive decor. Intimate and friendly atmosphere. Experienced personnel. Closed on Sunday.

⊚ Seafood

ISLAND OF MONTREAL

CRUSTACÉS (LES)
5706 Sherbrooke St. East, East End
(514) 256-2185
Cordial restaurant specializing in fresh seafood. Salad bar and varied menu. Musicians playing every evening.

FRIPON (LE)
436 Pl. Jacques Cartier, Old Montreal
(514) 861-1386
Parisian-style brasserie. Fine French cuisine specializing in seafood. Capacity of 400 with two reception rooms.

HOMARD FOU (LE)
403 Pl. Jacques Cartier, Old Montreal
(514) 398-9090
Restaurant with classic decor. Table d'hôte offered for lunch and dinner.

MAESTRO S.V.P.
3615 St. Laurent Blvd. (St. Lawrence), Plateau
(514) 842-6447
Seafood bistro with a mussels bar all year long. Table d'hôte offered at lunch. Casual and cordial ambiance. Capacity of 50 clients. Sliding doors open during the summer.

MER (LA)
1065 Papineau, Plateau
(514) 522-2889
Large restaurant and bistro. Specializing in seafood and grilled meats. Two floors with a capacity of 500 clients; three reception rooms. Table d'hôte includes an entrée, main dish, dessert and coffee. Different menu every day.

MOULERIE (LA)
1249 Bernard West, Mount Royal
(514) 273-8132
Restaurant specializing in mussels. Bistro-style. Friendly ambiance. Large terrasse of 105 places. Well situated establishment.

MOULES ET CIE
76 Roy, Plateau
(514) 496-0540
Intimate and casual ambiance. Specialties: mussels, fish and seafood. Specials vary according to the season.

PANORAMIQUE (LE)
250 St. Paul East, Old Montreal
(514) 861-1957
Charming romantic ambiance. French and Italian cuisine specializing in seafood. Table d'hôte offered all day.

POISSON ROUGE (LE)
1201 Rachel East, Plateau
(514) 522-4876
Large restaurant located opposite Lafontaine Park. Ideal for all special occasions. Table d'hôte at $32. Excellent quality/price ratio. Bring your own wine.

PÊCHE PÊCHE FISH & SEAFOOD
11598 de Salaberry, West Island
(514) 683-8601
Romantic and cordial ambiance. Fresh fish every three days. Specials for as little as $10. Reception room.

RESTAURANT DE LA PLACE ST-PAUL
262 St. Paul East, Old Montreal
(514) 874-7661
Romantic ambiance. Specializing in seafood and grilled meats. Two dining rooms. Fortification walls unique in town. Musicians in the summer.

RESTAURANT DU VIEUX PORT
39 St. Paul East, Old Montreal
(514) 866-3175
Large restaurant with eight reception rooms. Specializing in seafood and steaks. Table d'hôte offered everyday. European ambiance, room with a fireplace. Musicians on Fridays and Saturdays.

TERRAMARE

3633 Sources Blvd.,
West Island
(514) 683-4353
Restaurant specializing in grilled
meats, seafood and veal. Great
selection of dishes prepared with
care.

LAVAL & NORTH SHORE

HOMARD PLUS

3600 St. Martin West, Laval
(450) 688-7107
Restaurant of fine cuisine
specializing in seafood. Large
variety of dishes and all you can
eat specials during the week.
Excellent for romantic dinners.

PHARE DU NORD (LE)

1739 Blvd l'Avenir, Laval
(450) 688-9999
Warm atmosphere with a
traditional decor. Lobster pond
and a fresh fish counter. Daily
specials, table d'hôte and
catering service.

SOUTH SHORE

RESTAURANT LE YACHT

2264 rte. Marie-Victorin,
Longueuil
(450) 674-1444
Fine cuisine specializing in
seafood. Cordial atmosphere.
Decor similar to a boat cabin.
Table d'hôte is half price during
lunch.

RUSTIK

47 Blvd. St. Jean-Baptiste,
Chateuaguay
(450) 691-2444
Very particular ambiance.
Specializing in seafood and
steaks. Buffets. All kinds of
shows.

⊚ Spanish

CASA GALICIA (LA)

2087 St. Denis, Plateau
(514) 843-6698
Typical Spanish ambiance.
Specialties: paellas and various
seafood plates. Flamenco show
with musicians Fridays and
Saturdays. Table d'hôte during
lunch and dinner. Terrasse in the
summer.

CASA TAPAS

266 Rachel East, Plateau
(514) 848-1063
Typical Spanish decor. Very
cordial and modern ambiance.
Specializing in tapas. Open sliding
doors during the summer. Open
for over nine years. Reservations
are preferable.

DON MIGUEL

20 Prince Arthur West,
Plateau
(514) 845-7915
Family atmosphere and a Spanish
decor. Specializing in paellas.
Table d'hôte starting at $16.

EL GITANO

3507 Park Ave., Plateau
(514) 843-8212
Relaxed and cordial ambiance.
Typical Spanish cuisine
specializing in paellas and
seafood. Table d'hôte during
lunch for as little as $10.
Flamenco shows on Saturdays.
Open for over 30 years.

EL PATIO

425 Hickson, Downtown
(514) 766-5888
Spanish/Portuguese bistro that
serves tortillas, salads, squid and
grilled fish. Unpretentious and
calm ambiance.

SALA ROSSA

4848 St. Laurent Blvd.
(St. Lawrence), Plateau
(514) 844-4227
Located in the Spanish social
center building. Typical Spanish
cuisine specializing in tapas.
Flamenco dancers on Thursdays
from 10:30 pm and a jazz pianist
after the show. Concert hall on
the second floor.

◎ *Steak House*

ISLAND OF MONTREAL

BIFTÈQUE (LE)

6705 Côte de Liesse,
North End
(514) 739-6336
Recognized for over 15 years as
'the biggest beef steakhouse in
town'. A free meal for each 20
paid meals. Very roomy

restaurants (350 to 1 000 client
capacity) and ample parking.
Table d'hôte offered during lunch
and dinner. Special menus for
groups also available.

BOUCHERIE (LA)

343 St. Paul East,
Old Montreal
(514) 866-1515
Specialty: beef. Menu also
includes a good variety of fish,
lamb and seafood. Capacity of
140 clients. Singer on Thursdays
from May to June and in October.
Cordial ambiance, stone walls.

EL TORO

1647 Fleury East, North End
(514) 388-8676
Specialty: steaks. Beautiful
Mediterranean ambiance, two
fireplaces. Table d'hôte offered
during lunch and dinner.
Reception room and two parking
lots.

FIRESIDE

4759 Van Horne, Mount Royal
(514) 737-5576
Family restaurant, friendly and
courteous atmosphere.
Specialties: steaks and ribs. Good
fish selection. Table d'hôte
offered during lunch and dinner
includes entrée, main dish, coffee
and dessert. Open for over 16
years.

GRANDE MARQUISE

4134 Wellington, South End
(514) 769-4447
Family business. Specialties: fish
and ribs. Wooden decor.

JOE'S STEAKHOUSE

1430 Stanley, Downtown
(514) 842-4638
Family atmosphere and a cordial
ambiance. Great choice of dishes:
steaks, seafood, ribs and grilled
meats. Lunch specials for as little
as $10.

KEG (LE)

25 St. Paul East, Old Montreal
(514) 871-9093
Big restaurant. Specialty: steaks.
Nevertheless, the menu is varied.
Menu à la carte only. Adjacent
bar where one can buy Cuban
cigars.

MAISON DU BIFTECK ALOUETTE

1176 St. Catherine St. West,
Downtown
(514) 866-6244
Cordial ambiance. Specialty:
steaks with a penchant on fine
cuisine. Table d'hôte offered
during lunch and dinner includes
a soup, entrée, main dish and
coffee.

PEDDLERS

7500 Blvd. Newman,
South End
(514) 364-7204
Relaxed and friendly ambiance.
Table d'hôte and menu are
available every day.

RED GRILL STEAK HOUSE

349 Dorval, West Island
(514) 636-3599
Casual and cordial ambiance.
Specialties: steaks and seafood.
Table d'hôte includes a soup,
salad, main dish and coffee.
Reception room available.

STEAK & STEAK

5222 Sherbrooke St. East,
East End
(514) 255-5744
Specialties: steaks and seafood.
Casual and distinguished
ambiance. Table d'hôte offered
every day during lunch and
dinner. Children suppers Fridays
and Saturdays.
www.steaksteak.ca

VIEUX DULUTH (AU)

12856 Sherbrooke St. East,
East End
(514) 498-4886
Renowned for their generous
portions, excellent quality/price
value and an impeccable service.
The largest restaurant chain that
serves grilled meats and seafood
in Quebec. Ideal for family
outings or for outings between
friends or groups. Children's

menu is available. Bring your own wine.

VIEUX DULUTH (AU)
1997 Blvd. Marcel Laurin, North End
(514) 745-4525

VIEUX DULUTH (AU)
351 Duluth East, Plateau
(514) 842-5390

VIEUX DULUTH (AU)
3610 St. John's Blvd., West Island
(514) 624-0350

VIEUX DULUTH (AU)
5100 Sherbrooke St. East, East End
(514) 254-1347

VIEUX DULUTH (AU)
5600 Blvd. Henri Bourassa East, North End
(514) 326-7381

LAVAL & NORTH SHORE

HOUSTON STEAK ET CÔTES LEVÉES
407 Blvd. Labelle, Laval
(450) 971-7077
Cordial establishment. Shows from Thursday to Saturday. Private room for special occasions. Table d'hôte includes a soup or salad, main dish and tea or coffee.

MON VILLAGE
2760 ch. St. Charles, Hudson
(450) 458-5331
Courteous and rustic ambiance. Comprised of four private rooms, three fireplaces and a pub with its own menu. Brunches on Sundays. Children's menu available.

SAN ANTONIO
800 Blvd. Chomedey, Laval
(450) 682-7000
Cordial and quiet ambiance. Ten choices of tables d'hôtes between $10 and $30. Children's menu for as little as $6.

VIEUX DULUTH (AU)
999 Blvd. St. Martin West, Laval
(450) 629-1611
Renowned for their generous portions, excellent quality/price value and an impeccable service. The largest restaurant chain that serves grilled meats and seafood in Quebec. Ideal for family outings, or for outings between friends or groups. Children's menu is available. Bring your own wine.

SOUTH SHORE

BIFTÈQUE (LE)
100 Blvd. de Mortagne, Boucherville
(450) 449-3388
Recognized for over 15 years as 'the biggest beef steakhouse in town'. A free meal for each 20 paid meals. Very roomy

restaurants (350 to 1,000 client capacity) and ample parking. Table d'hôte offered during lunch and dinner. Special menus for groups also available.

HOUSTON STEAKS ET CÔTES LEVÉES

20 Blvd. de Mortagne, Boucherville

(450) 449-8777

Cordial establishment. Shows from Thursday to Saturday. Private room for special occasions. Table d'hôte includes a soup or salad, main dish, tea or coffee.

JACK ASTOR'S BAR & GRILL

3500 Taschereau Blvd., Greenfield Park

(450) 671-4444

Chicago deli with a 1950's ambiance. Varied menu: Mexican/Italian cuisine with steaks, grilled meats and chicken. Recognized as having the best fajitas on the South Shore. Bar with wine, beer and spirits.

STEAK & CIE

7845 Taschereau Blvd., Brossard

(450) 445-6231

Warm atmosphere with a fireplace during the winter. Table d'hôte offered during lunch and dinner; varied menu.

VIEUX DULUTH (AU)

3902 Taschereau Blvd., Greenfield Park

(450) 672-9921

Renowned for their generous portions, excellent quality/price value and an impeccable service. The largest restaurant chain that serves grilled meats and seafood in Quebec. Ideal for family outings, or outings between friends or groups. Children's menu is available. Bring your own wine.

ⓖ *Swiss*

ALPENHAUS*

1279 St. Marc, Downtown
(514) 935-2285
Fine Swiss and European style cuisine. Specialty: fondues. Rustic and romantic ambiance, including a fireplace and an old fashioned bar. Specials offered during lunch only. Two dining rooms and one private room.
Featured establishment see p. 186

CHEZ TRUDI

445 Lakeshore, West Island
(514) 631-1403
Fine European cuisine. Specialty: fondues. Rustic and cordial ambiance similar to a country cottage. Excellent quality/price value. Summer terrasse.

RACLETTE (LA)

1059 Gilford, Plateau
(514) 524-8118
Swiss and European style cuisine. Specialties: fondue and raclette.

Large variety of European dishes: duck, scallops, filet mignon, etc. Small and big table d'hôte, private room and a summer terrasse.

◎ *Tex/Mex*

CARLOS & PEPES

1420 Peel, Downtown
(514) 288-3090
Mexican and Californian cuisine. Typical ambiance, bar-style pub. Table d'hôte and happy hour during lunch and in the evening. Specialty: fajitas. Open sliding doors during the summer.

PLANÈTE (LE)

1451 St. Catherine St. East, East End
(514) 528-6953
World gastronomy with a touch of Californian cuisine. Modern and casual ambiance. Renowned for their grilled meats. Table d'hôte offered during lunch and dinner includes an entrée, main dish and coffee. Open sliding doors during the summer.

◎ *Thai*

BAN LAO-THAI

930 Decarie Blvd., Mount Royal
(514) 747-4805
Thai and Laotian cuisine. Typical Laotian ambiance. Specialty: papaya salad. Capacity of 36 clients.

BATÔ THAI

1310 St. Catherine St. East, East End
(514) 524-6705
Typical Thai ambiance. Capacity of 70 clients. Specialty: chicken with peanuts. Table d'hôte offered during lunch and dinner includes an entrée and main dish (dessert and coffee also offered during the evening).

CHANG THAI

2100 Crescent, Downtown
(514) 286-9994
High quality Thai cuisine. Exotic ambiance, with a variety of art pieces from Thailand. Diversified and refined menu. Table d'hôte offered during lunch. Reception room available.

CHAO PHRAYA

50 Laurier West, Plateau
(514) 272-5339
Large restaurant of fine cuisine. Traditional Thai ambiance. Open only during evenings. Table d'hôte offered during dinner.

CHU CHAI

4088 St. Denis, Plateau
(514) 843-4194
Restaurant offering a bistro style express section dedicated to take-out dishes. Thai ambiance. Specialty: vegetarian cuisine. Table d'hôte changes often.

CUISINE CHEF CHAUS

2437 Mount Royal East, Plateau
(514) 526-0230
Thai and Szechuan cuisine. Cordial ambiance with an aquarium. Table d'hôte offered during lunch and dinner.

PHAYATHAI

1235 Guy, Downtown
(514) 933-9949
Big two-floor restaurant of fine Thai cuisine. Typical ambiance, traditional music. Various tables d'hôtes offered each week but only offered during the day.

STE-ANNE SZECHUAN THAI

27 St. Anne, West Island
(514) 457-5366
Small restaurant of fine Thai and Szechuan cuisine. Romantic ambiance. Specialty: General Tao chicken. Table d'hôte and dinner for two specials available every day.

THAI GRILL

5101 St. Laurent Blvd. (St. Lawrence), Plateau
(514) 270-5566
Fine Thai cuisine. Rather modern ambiance. Bar and lounge, quite calm during the day. Specialty: grilled fish. A reception room for parties or groups is available.

THAI ORCHID

138 St. Paul East, Old Montreal
(514) 861-6640
Famous Thai restaurant. Separate sections for smokers and nonsmokers. Beautiful view of the Old Port. Table d'hôte for as little as $14 includes soup, rolls, main dish, dessert and coffee.

THAI-VIET

3610 St. Dominique, Plateau
(514) 288-5577
Fine Vietnamese and Thai cuisine. Diversified menu includes soups, grilled meats, noodles and other dishes. Terrasse with a capacity of 80 people open during the summer. Typical Asian decor. Bring your own wine.

THAÏLANDE

88 Bernard West, Plateau
(514) 271-6733
Fine cuisine with an exotic ambiance. Specialty: crispy duck. Table d'hôte offered during lunch and dinner includes a soup, salad, main dish, dessert and coffee.

⊚ *Tunisian*

COUSCOUSSIÈRE (LA)

1460 Amherst, East End
(514) 842-6667
Tunisian gastronomy which proposes a variety of couscous. Arab ambiance, traditional decor, small show. Attentive service. Baladi dancers on occasion.

KAMELA
1227 Marie Anne East, Plateau
(514) 526-0881
African cuisine, mostly specialties
from Tunisia. Try the egg 'brick'.
Good selection of couscous,
pizzas and pastas. Courteous
service.

KERKENNAH (LE)
1021 Fleury East, North End
(514) 387-1089
Restaurant of fine Tunisian
cuisine. Traditional ambiance with
Arab music. Lunch special for
business people. Good wine list.
Take-out service also available.

ÉTOILE DE TUNIS (L')
6701 de Chateaubriand,
North End
(514) 276-5518
Home-style cuisine. Family
restaurant with a casual
ambiance. Table d'hôte for two at
dinner starting at $39. Lunch for
as little as $11.

© *Vietnamese*

ISLAND OF MONTREAL

CAMÉLIA (LE)
5024 Côte des Neiges, Mount
Royal
(514) 738-8083
Small restaurant of fine cuisine
with a large variety of dishes:
Tonkinese soups, rolls, salads and
grilled meats. Vietnamese decor.
Table d'hôte available for dinner.

COIN D'ASIE
6020 Sherbrooke St. West,
West End
(514) 482-4035
Fine cuisine. Specialty:
Vietnamese fondue. Great
selection of grilled meats, salads,
soups and seafood. The lunch
special is different each day.
Asian ambiance and Vietnamese
musical instruments on the walls.

CRISTAL DE SAIGON
1068 St. Laurent Blvd. (St.
Lawrence), Downtown
(514) 875-4275
Authentic Vietnamese cuisine.
Pioneer of soup-meals *(phos)* in
Montreal. Open since 1984. Good
imperial rolls and fresh soups.
One of the rare restaurants to
offer egg noodle soup. Great
choice of soups. Try: Chinese
noodles and the beef soups.
Capacity of 30 clients.

ESCALE à SAIGON
107 Laurier West, Plateau
(514) 272-3456
Fine Vietnamese cuisine. Plush
and elegant ambiance. Great
selection of authentic Vietnamese
dishes served with an artistic
flair. Lunch specials and table
d'hôte include an entrée, main
dish with perfumed rice and a
dessert. Terrasse with a capacity
of 20 people.

ESTASIE

1320 St. Catherine St. East,
East End
(514) 598-1118
Menu composed of several
popular dishes: sushi, Thai,
Vietnamese and Indonesian
specialties. Refined cuisine
offering a variety of soups,
sautéed dishes and brochettes.

HARMONIE D'ASIE (L')

65 Duluth East, Plateau
(514) 289-9972
Open for over 15 years. Menu
includes imperial rolls and spring
rolls, vegetarian dishes and
several soups. Open from 5 pm
to 10 pm. Bring your own wine.

MANDOLINE (LA)

122 McGill, Old Montreal
(514) 397-4040
Dishes served with beautiful
presentations. Try their soup-
meals. Good choice of meats,
seafood, crispy noodles and
imperial rolls. Bistro-style decor.

MANGOUSTAN (LE)

5935 St. Hubert, North End
(514) 495-9031
Friendly restaurant, open for over
20 years. Specialties: lemon and
ginger soup, rice with chicken
and imperial rolls. Ambiance
without pretension.

MERVEILLE DU VIETNAM (LA)

4526 St. Denis, Plateau
(514) 844-9884
Renowned for several years for
the quality of their dishes and for
the courteousness of their
service. Varied menu composed
of entrées, grilled meats, an
impressive choice of sautéed
dishes and exotic desserts.
Delivery service available.

ONG CA CAN

79 St. Catherine St. East,
Downtown
(514) 844-7817
Fine Vietnamese cuisine.
Specialty: seven beef flavors
(dishes rolled in rice paste). Table
d'hôte can cost up to $30.
Capacity of 130 clients. Oriental
and modern decor.

PAPAYE VERTE (LA)

365 Bernard West,
Mount Royal
(514) 279-0688
Fine cuisine. Specialties: salads
and various preparations of green
papayas. Vietnamese ambiance.
Catering service available.
Refined dish presentations. Daily
special during lunch and table
d'hôte during the evening.

PHO BANG NEW YORK

1001 St. Laurent
(St. Lawrence) Blvd.
(514) 954-2032
Recently moved into a new
location. Bright, airy room

serving the best *pho* (beef soup with rice noodles) in the city. Great spring rolls, rice and noodle dishes. Authentic and incredibly affordable Vietnamese.

SOUVENIRS D'INDOCHINE

243 Mount Royal West, Plateau
(514) 848-0336
Fine cuisine, highly regarded for over 10 years. Varied menu: noodles, sautéed dishes, seafood, rolls, soups. Zen ambiance. Artistic clientele during the week and a more family clientele on weekends. Art exposition on occasion. Terrasse with view of the mountain.

THAO

2663 Ontario East, East End
(514) 522-5396
Vietnamese healthy cuisine. Specialty: Tonkinese soups. Menu includes won ton soups, snail dishes and a table d'hôte.

TRàNG AN

7259 St. Denis, North End
(514) 272-9992
Authentic Vietnamese restaurant. Healthy cuisine composed of *pho* soups, meats, salads and seafood.

LAVAL & NORTH SHORE

MAISON PHAM (LA)

610 Blvd. Cartier West, Laval
(450) 682-3659
Fine Vietnamese cuisine. Specialty: sautéed dishes. Elegant and plush decor; capacity of 75 clients. Table d'hôte offered during lunch and dinner. Friendly service.

ⓖ *World Cuisine*

AQUA TERRA

285 Mount Royal East, Plateau
(514) 288-3005
Market-style cuisine. Vast choice of dishes. Sushi counter. Table d'hôte during evenings only. Casual ambiance. Capacity of 60.

BABALOO

1864C Sources Blvd., West Island
(514) 695-6252
Stylish and entertaining ambiance. Orchestra on Wednesdays. Restaurant located close to Bourbon Street West: perfect for night outings. Table d'hôte during lunch and dinner. Great wine selection.

CENTAURE (LE)

7440 Decarie Blvd., Mount Royal
(514) 739-2741
Roomy restaurant located on the third floor of the Montreal Hippodrome Clubhouse. Capacity of 550 clients. Incredible view of the track and of Mount Royal. Free buffet and brunch for children under five years old and half price for children from six to twelve years old. Table d'hôte only on Wednesdays.

MARCHÉ MOVENPICK
1 Pl. Ville Marie, Downtown
(514) 861-4217
Restaurant that offers 12 different
styles of cuisines. Friendly and
lively ambiance. Dishes are
prepared in front of the
customers.

SOFIA
3600 St. Laurent Blvd.
(St. Lawrence), Plateau
(514) 284-0092
Restaurant-bar that serves pasta,
pizzas, steaks, fish, and seafood.
Animated lounge ambiance.
Stylish establishment. Table
d'hôte during the day and a
special of the day during the
evenings.

UN MONDE SAUTÉ
1481 Laurier East, Plateau
(514) 590-0897
Casual and warm ambiance.
Table d'hôte offered every day.
Specialties of the house:
Louisiana-style veal liver, ravioli
with wild mushrooms and fresh
fish. A well hidden treasure
worth trying.

Chapter 4. Nightclubs and Bars

Montreal is famous for its vibrant nightlife. An amazing array of bars and nightclubs cover virtually every type of night out one can wish to have. Whether looking for a low-key drink in a quiet bar or a huge club to dance the night away, Montreal will always have what you are looking for. The club and bar scene is massive and it would take several nights out to fully appreciate the broad spectrum of Montreal's nightlife.

Many bars, pubs and clubs insist on verifying age by checking identity cards if you look as though you are teetering on the legal drinking age, 18. Dress codes are location-specific. Most places are tolerant of dress, however, the more upscale bars and nightclubs insist on more formal attire (e.g. no jeans) and generally refuse clients that do not adhere to their dress code. Bars and nightclubs in Montreal are generally peaceful. Line-ups can be long depending on how *in* the establishment is, but the best thing about Montreal is there is always somewhere else to go.

Montreal is divided into nightlife neighbourhoods. Certain areas and, more specifically, streets hold the bulk of places where Montrealers spend their nights. These areas have a vast array of nightclubs, bars, pubs and lounges to satiate any preference.

Neighbourhoods & Times of Day

CRESCENT STREET

Crescent Street is the quintessential nightclub street. Between St. Catherine and de Maisonneuve, there is almost nothing but bars and nightclubs. It is the obvious destination for first-timers looking for a night out. On virtually every tourist guide, Crescent is cited as the street where nightlife is found. Mega-club establishments that have been around for decades pack in huge crowds every weekend, where the partying is aggressive and fun. The clubs on Crescent Street are very tourist-friendly and welcome out-of-town patronage. It was near here at **Grumpy's** (p. 165) (on Bishop south of St. Catherine) that Mordecai Richler and his regular crew would gather to drink and discuss weighty (and unweighty) topics. One of his *compadres*: columnist, city politician and well-known *bon vivant* Nick Auf der Maur even has a Crescent St. alley named after him (east side of Crescent, between St. Catherine and de Maisonneuve). The scene here is more corporate than other areas of the city, but that doesn't mean that good times are not to be had. First-time visitors to Montreal often come here to enjoy a pint at **Winnie's/Sir Winston's** (p. 166) or to go to the **Hard Rock Café** (p. 167). An interesting and welcome new arrival has been **Newtown** (p. 159), racing-car driver Jacques Villeneuve's night-club at de Maisonneuve and Crescent. 'Newtown' is his last name translated into English. It got him into trouble with the language police (the guardians of Quebec's language law, Bill 101), but a few years later the name and the establishment are both going strong. The street really comes into its own when Montreal's Formula One Grand Prix is happening (early June). The street is closed for pedestrian traffic and is packed with late night revelers. The area fills up with expensive sports cars and beautiful (and not-so-beautiful) people from across the globe. Regardless of the weekend, you'll always be able to find a good time on Crescent Street, as big and booming or as small and intimate as you desire. Within a two-block radius of Crescent Street, Montreal's best pubs can be found. **McKibbin's** (p. 166) is a great old-school Irish pub that has 3 floors of laid-back drinking. On certain nights, a full Celtic band can be found strumming away traditional Irish tunes. The vibe is friendly and easy. **Hurley's** (p. 165) is another Irish pub and hotspot. The crowd ranges in ages from 18 to 80. Food and darts can be had at any time of the day.

ST. LAURENT/ST. LAWRENCE BOULEVARD

St. Laurent Boulevard is the trendy strip, rife with the cool, the hip and the latest bars, lounges, restaurants and clubs. The clientele is an eclectic mix of the fashion forward, the trendy, hip artists, corporate cool guys and the raucous university crowd. On St. Laurent between Sherbrooke and Duluth, any and every type of night out can be enjoyed. This street is where Montreal goes to enjoy itself. Many restaurants turn into nightclubs at around eleven. Visiting stars, in town shooting a movie, spend most of their time at **Globe** (p. 167) on St. Laurent, a high-end restaurant that transforms into a watering hole for the rich, the seen and wanna-be-seen, the beautiful and those aching to get a peek at Leo Dicaprio or Ben Affleck. **Sofia** (p. 167) and **Cafeteria** are also restaurants that transform themselves into hotspots the moment the dining crowd has finished its desserts. Many of the female patrons jump up on the bar to show off their moves and themselves.

St. Laurent has a lot to offer. There are many great places to visit. **Tokyo Bar** (p. 160) has an incredible roof terrasse where you can drink the night away under the stars while watching the pedestrian traffic down below. **A Gogo Lounge** (p. 163) is a funky, 60's-inspired lounge that is always packed with beautiful people. **Café Méliès** (p. 155) is a quiet and beautifully designed lounge with an incredible laid-back feel that is a great place to hang out and spend a quieter night. **Bifteck** (p. 156) is another St. Laurent institution. Filled to the brim with the university crowd, the place is noisy and cheap, serving giant beers with complimentary popcorn. Bifteck is a great spot to visit on a night out for a drink and some ear numbing indie rock. **Le Swimming** (p. 164) is a pool bar that has transformed itself into an amazing spot to see local bands perform. If you are a lover of music and into getting a taste of Montreal's burgeoning music scene, Le Swimming is a must. Other great places to visit on St. Laurent are **Blizzarts** (p. 163), **Buddha Bar** (p. 163) and **Blue Dog** (p. 167).

CINQ À SEPT

Montreal's own version of happy hour is referred to as *cinq à sept*, which, directly translated, means five to seven. Like a lot of things in Montreal, this term can be a bit of a misnomer: sometimes the action only gets going around 7 pm. These are very popular all over Montreal and you can always find a huge crowd of people trying to unwind after a hard day's work. There are many places to go, but among the best is **Mile End Bar** (p. 163) on St. Laurent near Fairmount. The crowd is varied, boisterous and fun. Drink specials range from cheap 2-for-1 specials, specials on local beer and reduced rates for cocktails. A new *cinq à sept* addition to the city is **W** (p. 164). It is expensive, trendy – and popular.

THE REST

There are many other streets to visit that have a great number of bars, pubs and clubs. Laurier Street has **Sofa** (p. 162), a laid-back lounge with an older, more professional crowd. Ontario Street has **Jello Bar** (p. 164), a great spot for martinis and live music. St. Denis has the infamous **St-Sulpice** (p. 157), which features a giant terrasse that is always packed with a mostly francophone crowd. **Bily Kun** (p. 165) is another great spot on Mount Royal near St. Denis which features an incredible selection of amazing local brews and always an interesting and funky crowd.

Whatever your tastes, Montreal's nightlife is varied enough to cater to any desire, thirst, or need. The best way to get a proper taste of Montreal's nightlife is to be adventurous. The best (non-book) guides to Montreal's nightlife tend to be those people working in the bars and restaurants. Don't be shy to ask them where they go out and spend their evenings. More often than not, they'll let you in on a little secret spot that you would never find without some inside dope.

WHAT TO DRINK

Drinks of whatever kind help make or break a night. Suggesting moderation may be out of place, but always makes the 'morning after' a lot smoother. When ordering drinks in this city, Montrealers are in two camps. The old stand-bys of beer and alcohol with mix are great for the taverns and the local casual spots. Microbrews and premium drinks are more suited for a night in hot local supper clubs and discos. Red and white wines can be of the boxed variety behind the bar, although of late certain nightspots offer several selections by the glass depending on their level of food service. Many of the Plateau and Mile End bars also double as restaurants. The more elegant the décor, the more likely you can order a good glass of red, an impressive white and even French and Californian bubbly. Hot drinks at the moment are the Mojito, scotches of varying intensities, Lychee martinis, Caiparina and the standards of the 40's like the Collins, Bombay Sapphire and tonic and the Manhattan. For extensive wine and cocktail lists in a great ambiance try **Cafe Méliès** (p. 155), **Savannah** (p. 94) and **W** (p. 164).

◎ *Afterhour*

Aria
1280 St. Denis
(514) 987-6712

Red light
1955 Notre Dame de Fatima
(450) 967-3057

◎ *Bar*

Bar Taboo
1950 Blvd de Maisonneuve
East
(514) 597-0010

Bar Chez Clo Clo
2461 Bélanger St.
(514) 727-0308

Bar Chez Monique
937 12th Ave.
(450) 439-2121

Bar Derek
5817 St-Laurent
(514) 948-1431

Bar Exxxotica
5169 Park Ave.,
(514) 272-4744

Bar Laurier
5141 St. Denis
(514) 276-0214

Bar Le Gogue
4177 St. Denis St.
(514) 845-8717

Bifteck
3702 St. Laurent
(514) 844-6211

Cafe Soho
6289 St. Hubert St.
(514) 271-3006

Cheers
1260 Mackay
(514) 932-3138

Club Date Piano-Bar
1218 St. Catherine St. East
(514) 521-1242

Club Nexxt
1635 St-Laurent St.
(514) 849-6398

Copacabana
3910 St. Laurent Blvd.
(514) 982-0880

Green Room/Salon Vert
5386 St. Laurent
(514) 495-4448

L'Intrus Café Bar
1351 Rachel East
(514) 523-6447

Jupiter Room
3874 St. Laurent

Korova
3908 St. Laurent
(514) 848-0343

L'Escogriffe
4467A St. Denis
(514) 842-7244

Loft
1405 St. Laurent
(514) 281-8058

St-Sulpice
1680 St. Denis
(514) 844-9458

Zebra Bar
179 Jean Talon West
(514) 270-0475

◎ *Cigar Lounges*

Cigare Club Etcetera
4115 St. Denis
(514) 281-0225

Stogies
2015 Crescent
(514) 848-0069

◎ *Comedy*

Comedy Nest
2313 St. Catherine St. West
(Pepsi Forum)
(514) 932-6378

Comedy Works
1238 Bishop
(514) 398-9661

◎ *Country*

Club Bolo
960 Amherst
(514) 849-4777

Spurs
7360 St-Jacques W.
(514) 484-3641

Zoo Lounge
4061 Ontario E.
(514) 523-3344

◎ *Dance Club*

980 (Le)
980 Rachel East St
(514) 596-3981

737
1 Place Ville-Marie, PH2
(514) 397-0737

Bar 1250
1250 Roberval St
(450) 653-1900

Bar Vision
7216 Newman Blvd.
(514) 366-8073

Barber Shop Disco Bar
1400 Edouard Blvd
(450) 678-0710

Belmont
4483 St. Laurent Blvd.
(514) 845-8443

Central Ganesh
 4479 Saint Denis
(514) 845-9010

Central Station
4432 St. Laurent
(514) 842-2836

Club Balattou
4372 St. Laurent Blvd.
(514) 845-5447

Club Extreme
2020 Crescent
(514) 288-2582

Club La Boom Montreal
1254 Stanley
(514) 866-5463

Coconut Groove
5312 Levesque E.
(450) 661-6444

Diable Vert
4557 St. Denis
(514) 849-5888

Dome
32 Ste-Catherine W.
(514) 875-5757

El Zaz Bar
4297 St. Denis St.
(514) 288-9798

Electric Avenue
1469 Crescent
(514) 285-8885

Flash Back
1600 Robinson
(450) 688-6490

Funkytown club disco
1454 Peel
(514) 282-8387

Fuzzy Bar
1600 St. Martin Blvd East,
Laval
(450) 669-2404

Fuzzy Bar
3 du Commerce Pl, Brossard
(450) 466-6877

High Bar
1635 St. Laurent
(514) 288-6171

Jet Nightclub
1003 St. Catherine St. East
(514) 842-2582

Joy
2102 Mountain (de la
Montagne)
(514) 287-1177

Kamasutra Club
3580 St. Dominique
(514) 842-4892

Karina
1455 Crescent, 2nd Floor
(514) 288-0616

L'Action Disco Club
4645 Metropolitain East
(514) 727-3749

Living (Le)
4521 St. Laurent
(514) 286-9986

London
3523A St. Laurent
(514) 288-4994

Millennium Club
7500 Viau
(514) 721-4949

Moomba
1780 Pierre-Peladeau Ave
(450) 973-7787

Newtown
1476 Crescent
(514) 284-6555

Night Club Castel
1423 Crescent
(514) 849-8870

Orchid
3556 St. Laurent
(514) 848-6398

Passeport
4156 St. Denis St.
(514) 842-6063

Pop
1008 Ste-Catherine E.
(514) 859-9052

Saphir
3699 St. Laurent
(514) 284-5093

Select Bar Rencontre
5800 Metropolitain Blvd.
(514) 251-7658

Sugar (Le)
3616 St. Laurent Blvd
(514) 287-6555

Thursdays
1449 Crescent
(514) 288-5656

Time
997 St. Jacques West
(514) 392-9292

Tokyo
3709 St. Laurent
(514) 842-6838

Tops (Laval)
1545 Corbusier
(450) 973-8677

Upper Club
3519 Saint Laurent Blvd.
(514) 285-4464

Vatican
1432 Crescent
(514) 845-3922

Wax Lounge
3481 St. Laurent
(514) 282-0919

Zinc Bar Tabac
1148 av Mont-Royal E.
(514) 523-5432

◎ *Folk Music*

Deux Pierrots
104 St-Paul E.
(514) 861-1270

Pierrot (le)
114 St-Paul E.
(514) 861-1270

◎ *Gay*

Agora
1160 Mackay
(514) 934-1428

Backtrack
1592 Ste- Catherine East
(514) 523-4679

Citi-Bar
1603 Ontario E.
(514) 525-4251

Drugstore
1366 Ste-Catherine E.
(514) 524-1960

Meteor
1661 Ste-Catherine E.
(514) 523-1481

Saloon Café
1333 Ste-Catherine E.
(514) 522-1333

Sky Pub
1474 Ste-Catherine E.
(514) 529-6969

West Side
1017 cote du Beaver Hall
(514) 866-4963

◎ *Jazz & Blues*

Autre Bar
278 Laurier W
(514) 278-1519

Barfly
4062A St. Laurent
(514) 993-5154

Biddles Jazz & Ribs
2060 Aylmer
(514) 842-8656

Café Sarajevo
2080 Clark
(514) 284-5629

Upstairs Jazz Bar & Grill
1254 Mackay
(514) 931-6808

◎ *Karaoke*

Bar Chez Pier O
230 Principale St, St. Sauveur
(450) 227-6005

Bar Vocalz
1421 Crescent
(514) 288-9119

Laser Star Karaoke Bar
2151 Mountain (de la
Montagne)
(514) 844-1791

Tycoon
96 Sherbrooke St. W.
(514) 849-8094

◎ *Latino Music*

Cactus
4461 St. Denis
(514) 849-0349

Copacabana
1106 Maisonneuve W.
(514) 282-7787

Salsathèque
1220 Peel
(514) 875-0016

Tango Libre
1650 Marie Anne E.
(514) 527-5197

◎ *Live Band Bar*

Bar L'Essentiel
25 Grande Cote Rd.,
Boisbriand
(450) 433-1311

Bar Chez Francoise
3785 St. Catherine St. East.
(514) 527-8198

Bistro à Jojo
1627 St. Denis
(514) 843-5015

Bobards
4328 St. Laurent
(514) 987-1174

Bourbon Street West
1866 Sources
(514) 695-6545

Cabaret Music Hall
2111 St. Laurent
(514) 845-2014

Café Campus
57 Prince Arthur E.
(514) 844-1010

Casa del Popolo
4873 St. Laurent
(514) 284-0122

Divan Orange (Le)
4234 St. Laurent
(514) 840-9090

Foufounes Electriques
87 St. Catherine E.
(514) 844-5539

Jello Bar
151 Ontario E.
(514) 285-2621

Kola Note
5240 Park Ave.
(514) 274-9339

Medley
1170 St. Denis
(514) 842-6557

Ours qui fume (blues)
2019 St. Denis
(514) 845-6998

Sofa
451 Rachel East
(514) 285-1011

Toc Toc
6091 Parc
(514) 575-0014

Velvet Club (le)
420 St-Gabriel
(514) 878-9782

@ *Lounge*

A Gogo Lounge
3682 St. Laurent
(514) 286-0882

Blizzarts
3956A St. Laurent (St.
Lawrence) Boulevard
(514) 843-4860

Brandy
21 St-Paul East
(514) 871-9178

Buddha Bar (Le)
3616 St. Laurent (St.
Lawrence) Boulevard
(514) 287-6555

Cabaret
Hotel de la Montagne
(514) 288-5656

Cristallin
Hotel Inter. Continental – 360
St. Antoine West
(514) 987-9900

Enoteca
7112 boul St. Laurent
(514) 276-7475

Finnegan & Bacchus
1458 Mountain (de la
Montagne)
(514) 842-8825

Havana Lounge
357 St-Charles W.
(450) 670-2626

Hotel de la Montagne
1430 Mountain (de la
Montagne)
(514) 288-5656

Hypertaverne Edgar
1562 av Mt-Royal E.
(514) 521-4661

Luba Lounge
2109 Bleury
(514) 288-5822

Magellan
330 Ontario East.
(514) 845-0909

Mile End Bar
5322 St. Laurent
(St. Lawrence) Boulevard
(514) 279-0200

Spirite lounge
1209 Ontario East.
(514) 522-5353

W Hotel
901 Square Victoria
(514) 395-3100

Winnie's
1455 Crescent
(514) 288-0623

◎ *Pool halls*

Bacci
4205 St. Denis
(514) 844-3929

Baloos
403 Ontario East.
(514) 843-5469

Bar Billard Le Plateau Mont-Royal
1673 Mont-Royal
(514) 526-8858

Istori
486 Ste-Catherine West.
(514) 396-2299

Metropool
1197 St. Laurent
(514) 392-1458

RackNRoll Bar Billard
551 ac Mont-Royal E.
(514) 525-5091

Sharx Pool
1606 Ste-Catherine W.
(514) 934-3105

Le Skratch
1875 Panama Ave.,
South Shore
(450) 466-7903

Le Skratch West Island
11829 Bd Pierrefonds, West
Island
(514) 683-5000

Le Skratch
7803 Newman Blvd.,
South End
(514) 595-7665

Le Skratch
965, Curé Labelle Blvd., Laval
(450) 686-7665

Swimming
3643 St. Laurent
(514) 282-7665

Trix
1500 Atwater
(514) 934-2434

@ *Pub*

Amere a Boire
2049 St. Denis
(514) 282-7448

Andrews Pub
1241 Guy St.
(514) 932-4584

Bières & Compagnie
3547 St. Laurent
(514) 288-0210

Bières & Compagnies
4350 St. Denis
(514) 844-0394

Bily Kun
354 Mont-Royal East
(514) 845-5392

Boudoir
850 Mont-Royal E.
(514) 526-2819

Brasserie Lachine
2300 32e Ave
(514) 631-4343

Brutopia
1219 Crescent
(514) 393-9277

Cheval Blanc
809 Ontario East.
(514) 522-0211

Claddagh Pub
1433 Crescent
(514) 287-9354

Cock n Bull
1944 Ste-Catherine West.
(514) 933-4556

Futenbulle
273 Bernard West
(514) 276-0473

Gerts
3480 McTavish
(514) 398-3001

Grumpy's
1242 Bishop
(514) 866-9010

Hurley's Irish Pub
1225 Crescent
(514) 861-4111

Ile Noire
342 Ontario E.
(514) 982-0866

James Rooster Esq.
3 de la Commune
(514) 842-3822

Jillys
6900 Decarie
(514) 738-2299

Madhatter
1220 Crescent
(514) 987-9988

Magnan Restaurant & Taverne
2602 St-Patrick
(514) 935-9647

McKibbin's Irish Pub
1426 Bishop St.
(514) 288-1580

McKibbin's—The Toucan
1426 Bishop St (above McKibbins)
(514) 288-1580

Mclean's Pub
1210 Peel
(514) 393-3132

Musée de la Biere a Montreal
2063 Stanley
(514) 840-2020

Olde Orchard Pub & Grill
5563 Monkland, West End
(514) 484-1569

Peel Pub
1107 Ste Catherine W.
(514) 844-6769

Pub St-Paul
124 St-Paul East
(514) 874-0485

Quai des Brumes
4481 St. Denis
(514) 499-0467

Quartier Latin Pub
318 Ontario E.
(514) 845-3301

Sergent Recruteur
4650 St. Laurent
(514) 287-1412

Sir Winston Churchill Pub
1459 Crescent
(514) 288-0623

Ste-Elizabeth
1412 Ste-Elizabeth
(514) 286-4302

Verre Bouteille
2112 av Mt-Royal E.
(514) 521-9409

Old Dublin
1219a University
(514) 861-4448

Ziggy's
1470 Crescent
(514) 285-8855

◎ *Resto Bar*

Barraca
1134 Mont Royal East

Bar Satellite Dorval
365 Dorval Ave
(514) 422-0070

Hard Rock Café
1458 Crescent
(514) 987-1420

Laïka
4040 St. Denis
(514) 842-8088

Manago
330 Ste-Catherine E.
(514) 845-5505

Pub St. Cimboire
1693 St. Denis
(514) 843-6360

Shed Café
3515 St. Laurent
(514) 842-0220

◎ *Resto Club*

Buona Notte
3518 St. Laurent
(514) 848-0644

Globe
3455 St. Laurent
(514) 284-3823

Sofia
3600 St. Laurent
(514) 284-0092

◎ *Singles Bars*

Lovers
1989 Autoroute 440, Laval
(450) 682-2020

Lovers
5440 Sherbrooke St. E.
(514) 253-3030

Lovers
8245 Taschereau, Brossard
(450) 445-2525

◎ *Social Dancing*

Blue Dog
3958 St. Laurent
(514) 848-7006

Doremi
505 Belanger St. E
(514) 274-5456

Alphabetical Index

Index by Area

BISTRO UNIQUE, 68
CAFE ET BOUFFE, 73
CANTINA (LA), 103
CHEZ BONNIN, 85
COIN DU MEXIQUE (LE), 128
COLBERT (LE), 69
DEUX CHEFS (LES), 100
DI LUSSO, 105
ECHE PA' ECHARLA, 128
EL CHALAN, 128
EL JIBARO, 128
ETOILE DE TUNIS (L'), 146
EUGENIO, 106
GAVROCHE (LE), 86
GOELETTE (LA), 81
IRAZU, 128
LAS PALMAS PUPUSERIA, 31, 128
MANGOUSTAN (LE), 147
MELCHORITA, 128
PIANO PIANO, 112
ROBERTO, 114
TRANG AN, 148
TRATTORIA, 115

SOUTH END
ST. HENRI
AMBIANCE, 99
MICHAEL W., 27, 42, 87
QUATRE SAISONS, 127
SANS MENU, 71
VERDUN/LASALLE
AMALFITANA (L'), 102
AREA, 94
BATÒ THAI, 144
CASA GRECQUE, 29, 94
CHEZ PIERRE, 85
CIOCIARA (LA), 104
COPINES DE CHINE, 75
COUSCOUSSIÈRE (LA), 145
CUCINA LINDA RISTORANTE, 104
D'AMICHI, 46, 104

DELICES DE L'ILE MAURICE, 24, 30
DIVA (LA), 46, 105
ESTASIE, 147
GRAIN DE SEL (LE), 69
GRANDE MARQUISE, 141
INDEPENDANT (L'), 87
MER (LA), 130, 138
MIYAKO, 124
PARADIS DES AMIS (LE), 74
PEDDLERS, 141
PETIT EXTRA (AU), 71
PICCOLO DIAVOLO, 112
PLANÈTE (LE), 144
PREMIÈRE (LA), 95
SPIRITE LOUNGE, 163
TRATTORIA AUX 3 CONTINENTS, 115

EAST END
ANJOU/ST. LEONARD
BÂTON ROUGE, 65
CHERO, 127
DI MENNA, 105
EAST SIDE MARIO'S, 106
FONDUES DU ROI (LES), 82
FOUR DE ST- LEONARD (LE), 107
GIORGIO, 107
IL PAZZESCO, 109
MOE'S DELI & BAR, 80
RIBERA, 113
RISTORANTE FRESCO, 113
STEAK FRITES ST-PAUL, 56
TRATTORIA DEL GALLO NERO, 115
VIEILLE CHEMINEE (A LA), 116
HOCHELAGA-MAISONNEUVE
BECANE ROUGE (LA), 84
BENI HANA GRILL, 123
CASA GRECQUE, 29

CHEZ BEAUCHESNE, 85
CHEZ CLO, 156
CRUSTACES (LES), 137
DORA (LA), 105
JOLI MOULIN (LE), 87
KOBE STEAKHOUSE, 124
MOE'S DELI & BAR, 80-81
PERLA (LA), 111
RESTAURANT BISTRO L'ADRESSE, 71
RIVOLI, 82
STEAK & STEAK, 141
VIEUX DULUTH (AU), 32, 141
WAH-DO, 79
MONTREAL EAST
AL CAPRICCIO, 102
FLAMBERGE (LA), 100
GIORGIO, 107
MER JAUNE (LA), 76
NOUVEAU PARADIS (LE), 77
PETITE VENISE (LA), 112
PRIMA LUNA, 112
RESTAURANT AUBERGE DU CHEVAL BLANC, 89
THAO, 148
VIEUX DULUTH (AU), 32, 141

WEST END
NOTRE-DAME-DE-GRÂCE
AL DENTE, 102
ANTICO MARTINI, 102
BENEDICTS, 73
CAVEAU SZECHWAN (LE), 74
COIN D'ASIE, 146
HWANG-KUM, 127
ITALIANO, 120
LOUISIANE (LA), 73
MAISTRE (LE), 87
MESSOB D'OR (AU), 64
MONKLAND TAVERN, 136
PASTA CASARECCIA, 111
SUL AC JUNG, 127

Alpenhaus

1279 St . Mark,
just west of downtown (Downtown)
(514) 935-2285

Alpenhaus is located between downtown Montreal and Westmount in Shaughnessy Village. The restaurant recently celebrated its 38th anniversary.

Alpenhaus is a romantic restaurant that offers authentic fondues, as well as other excellent European dishes. From the moment one enters the restaurant, the ambiance is typical of a Swiss *auberge*. There is a choice of two dining rooms. The principal one features an ensemble of murals, weapons, stained glass and tapestries evocative of medieval Europe. The other dining room (open from Friday to Sunday only) is the Heidi Room: a large space that proudly displays the canton of Aargau's standard. This room, heated by fireplace and featuring a piano, is the perfect setting for a romantic evening.

Like Switzerland itself, Swiss cuisine combines German, Italian and French influences. A Swiss dinner can start with raclette, a dish that melted cheese lovers will appreciate. Raclette is composed of melted cheese, served over potatoes with lots of ground black pepper, accompanied by small pickled onions and pickles. The name comes from the French word *racler*, to scrape, because of the way the cheese is scraped from the block. Others can enjoy an entrée of Grisons meat, followed by a traditional three-cheese onion soup or a lightly spiced goulash.

The sommelier can advise you what wine will best complement your choice of meat. Many will choose the Alpenhaus merlot. In the beer department, there are several Swiss (e.g. Swiss Mountain) and other European beers (e.g. Tuborg) to choose from.

Of course, fondue itself must not be forgotten. To sample a number of different types at one sitting, order the Fondue Festival. It combines Chinese, Swiss, and bourguignon fondue and, for dessert, includes chocolate fondue. Connoisseurs may prefer the rack of lamb with mint jelly.

To finish the meal, choose the chocolate fondue, the crème caramel, or a fruit salad with ice cream.

A touch of Switerland in Montreal – not to be missed.

Sho-Dan

2020 Metcalfe, Downtown
(514) 987-9987
1425 René Levesque Blvd.
(fka Dorchester), Downtown
(514) 871-0777
www.sho-dan.com

As North Americans have become more focused on health, Japanese cuisine has grown in popularity. As a result, it is no surprise to find several Japanese and sushi restaurants in Montreal, but few can rival **Sho-Dan**.

The two Sho-Dan locations have a modern ambiance perfect for a cosmopolitan city like Montreal. The service is attentive and focused on creating the right atmosphere.

At noon, the clientele is composed of business people; in the evening, a more diverse group enjoys the

Black Dragon

tranquil atmosphere created by the subdued lighting and elegant choice of furniture. Sho-Dan features Asian, jazz-influenced music and deserves its reputation as a chic sushi bar. Two private rooms can seat a total of 24 people and a sushi bar surrounds the main dining room.

The menu is accessible, but innovative and ever-changing. There are several house specialties, including sushi pizza (tuna, smoked salmon, caviar and rice cake), the Rose Maki (tempura shrimp with red tuna, avocado, lemon mayonnaise and asparagus) and the Black Dragon (spicy tuna with mango). These dishes are perfect for those who prefer cooked fish. Customers can choose a wine to accompany their meal from Sho-Dan's extensive wine list.

Sho-Dan is a wonderful Japanese restaurant. Its elegant and refined atmosphere is the product of Japanese cuisine evolving in a North American context.

Both Sho-Dan locations are located in the heart of downtown Montreal.

Rose Maki

Stash Café
200 Rue St. Paul, Old Montreal
(514) 845-6611
www.stashcafe.com

Stash Café is located in the heart of Old Montreal in a building typical of the neighbourhood. Although less ancient than its surroundings, the restaurant has deep roots in Montreal.

In 1972, Stanislaw Pruszynski opened one of Montreal's first flea markets. The market was successful and became a well-known meeting place for artists. Over time, Stanislaw began to make soup for his customers – and the ancestor of the Stash Café was born. Several years later, Eva Bujnicka founded the current restaurant. Twenty-five years after that, the

restaurant moved to Rue St. Paul in Old Montreal and changed its name to Stash Café – 'Stash' being a short form of 'Stanislaw'. Today, Stash Café is one of the best Polish restaurants in Montreal. The restaurant evokes the pre-World War II era: the atmosphere is subdued and a pianist plays every day, starting at 6 pm.

No Polish meal can begin without a taste of vodka and Stash Café has three Polish varieties to offer. A common favourite: Zubrowka – a vodka flavoured with bison grass.

The menu is typically Polish and includes meals from all parts of the country. All the dishes are prepared in the traditional Polish manner. There are game meats such as *bigos*, a cabbage stew with meat, sausages and wild mushrooms. There are also better-known Polish specialties such as *pierogi* – dumplings filled with meat, cheese or cabbage – best eaten with sour cream. *Placki* are potato pancakes served with sour cream and apple sauce. Another pancake dish, *krokiety* (pancake rolls filled with meat), is simple but tasty. *Golabki* (stuffed cabbage served with potatoes and vegetables) represents the finest of traditional home-style Polish cuisine.

The restaurant is a glimpse of Poland in Montreal. Visit it to find out how it has bridged the gap between these two places.